Canal Parks, Museums and Characters of the Mid-Atlantic

Kate Mulligan

Wakefield Press
Washington, D.C.

First published in 1999 by Wakefield Press,
P.O. Box 23392, Washington, D.C. 20026

ISBN 0-9655552-1-6

Library of Congress Catalog Card Number 99-71418

Cover and Page Design by Scott Edie, E Graphics, Brunswick, MD

Acknowledgments

Thanks to many people who offered information and interview leads. Particular thanks to those who reviewed all or part of the book: Jim Amon, Linda and Robert Barth, Tom Hahn, Mike High, Keith Melder and Lance Metz.

Map credits: (10) The Pennsylvania Canals historic leaflet, published by the Pennsylvania Historical and Museum Commission; (14) E Graphics; (33) E Graphics; (56) E Graphics; (92) Canal Society of New Jersey.

Photo credits: (17) George Harvan from collection of National Canal Museum (NCM); (19) NCM; (21) courtesy of the Library of Congress (LC); (25) J.E.B. Elliott (NCM); (29) courtesy of the Switchback Railroad Foundation; (31) J.E.B. Elliott (NCM); (41) (LC); (43) (c)1998, Eastern National. Reprinted with permission; (64) Jack Rottier, National Park Service, The Gelman Library, George Washington University; (65) Hal Larsen; (68) Kate Mulligan; (71) Kate Mulligan; (74) Kate Mulligan; (75) Kate Mulligan; (76) courtesy of U.S. Army Corps of Engineers (ACE); (78) (ACE); (84) (ACE); (87) courtesy of Susquehanna Museum of Havre de Grace at the Lockhouse; (108) James C. Amon; (109) Robert H. Barth; (111) (LC).

Cover credits: George Harvan, Library of Congress, National Canal Museum and Jack Rottier.

Table of Contents

Introduction

I began this book with a simple objective: to provide basic information for the casual visitor about canal parks and museums in the mid-Atlantic region. My interest grew out of my experience promoting an earlier book, *Towns along the Towpath*, which describes the impact of the Chesapeake and Ohio Canal as it traveled to western Maryland and tells of the long struggle to turn the canal area into a national park.

I learned that the Chesapeake and Ohio Canal National Historic Park is only one of a growing number of parks and museums that celebrate canal life. In 1988, Congress created the Illinois and Michigan Canal National Heritage Corridor as the first of a new breed of national park and has since designated canal heritage corridors in Pennsylvania, Rhode Island, Georgia and Ohio. The new National Canal Museum is bringing crowds to Easton, Pennsylvania and the famed New York State Canal System continues to expand and improve its 500 plus miles of navigable waterways and towpath trails. The Delaware and Raritan Canal has become one of New Jersey's primary attractions.

I also got to know members of canal societies. Fan is too tame a word to describe these passionate advocates who do everything from picking up trash to designing museum exhibits and lobbying public officials. Virtually every canal is associated with a legendary figure who walked every inch of a towpath or park in order to produce a guidebook.

My new book was still under control until I ventured into the Library of Congress to look into the origins of Mid-Atlantic canals. Accounts of canal building offer a wonderful entry to one of the most intriguing periods of American history and I soon became hooked by the struggles to develop the young country.

Canals were a major preoccupation of many early leaders. Before he was president of the country, George Washington was president of the Patowmack Company, which built a series of short canals. John Quincy Adams said it was the greatest moment of his life, when he dug into the ground to begin construction of the Chesapeake and Ohio Canal. Nearly 100 years before the Revolutionary War, William Penn proposed a canal to link Philadelphia with western Pennsylvania.

Canal building also attracted a terrific set of less familiar characters. Josiah White, a Pennsylvania entrepreneur, survived fire, flood and financial ruin to create a transportation empire. Mathew Carey fled from a prison term in his native Ireland;

worked with Benjamin Franklin in Paris; built the country's first modern publishing company; lobbied on behalf of orphans, prisoners and other outcasts and still found time to promote the Pennsylvania Mainline Canal. Canal engineer John Randel, Jr., won a legal suit against the Chesapeake and Delaware Canal company for $250,000, at a time when canal company presidents made about $2,000 annually.

These larger- than- life characters operated in a world where everything seemed possible. In 1816, when New Yorkers decided to build the 363-mile Erie Canal, the longest canal in the country was less than a tenth that length. Their Pennsylvania counterparts set about building a canal from Philadelphia to Pittsburgh without a plan for getting canal boats over the Allegheny Mountain. The 102-mile Morris Canal in New Jersey conquered a rise and fall that totaled nearly 1,700 feet. Canal companies underestimated costs; went bankrupt; borrowed money and pushed on.

A canal was the impetus for the famous report on internal improvements from Albert Gallatin, the Secretary of the Treasury. John Adams, then a congressman, asked the Secretary to recommend whether Congress should appropriate funds for the Chesapeake and Delaware Canal and other internal improvements. In 1808, Gallatin offered a lucid defense for the controversial step of federal involvement in building the country's infrastructure. "Good roads and canals will shorten distances, facilitate commercial and personal intercourse, and unite, by a still more intimate community of interests, the most remote quarters of the United States."

Against my will, the book became more complicated. I decided to write about some of the 19th-century figures who were responsible for the triumphs of the canal era and to tell the stories of our 20th-century heroes and heroines who led the efforts for canal restoration. You'll find vignettes of some of my favorite canal characters scattered among the maps, pictures and descriptions of canal parks. I also added descriptions of sites and museums that will help put canal building in a historic context.

Anyone who has spent even an afternoon hiking or biking along a towpath has probably felt an elementary version of canal magic. I hope this book encourages you to stop for awhile, look around a canal museum or join a park ranger for a talk about the push westward by waterway. For those willing to glance back, canals offer a wonderful passage to the pivotal time when the country began to abandon its agrarian past and embrace the challenges of industrialization

THE CANAL ERA

The Erie Canal opened on October 26, 1825 with the biggest celebration American had ever seen. De Witt Clinton, New York's governor and the canal's most energetic advocate, took his place on the *Seneca Chief*, the lead boat in a flotilla that would travel from Buffalo to Albany and down the Hudson River to New York City. In the boat's cabin were two kegs painted in patriotic designs and filled with water from Lake Erie.

Cannons were spaced at 8- to 10-mile intervals along the route. The departure of the *Seneca Chief* was announced with a volley of cannon fire, which was echoed by the next cannon, until the news finally reached New York City 80 minutes later. Barges, steamboats, ships, pilot boats and canal boats joined the flotilla as it moved past cheering crowds. Thirty thousand out-of-towners and almost the entire population of New York City met the boats and followed them to Sandy Hook for another ceremony.

Clinton poured the contents of the kegs into the Atlantic Ocean for the first Wedding of the Waters ceremony and then added the contents of vials of water from the Ganges, Thames, Nile and Seine. Yet another blast of cannon fire signaled the opening of a gigantic parade, which was followed by balls, parties and banquets. The legacy of this 10-day extravaganza lingered for years. Babies, boats, locomotives and anything else that could be christened were given the name De Witt Clinton.

A canal was not a new concept. In fact, it was a subject of speculation as early as 1673, when Louis Joliet envisioned a water connection between Lake Michigan and the Illinois River. Three years later, colonists thought of cutting a channel through a narrow neck of land on Cape Cod. George Washington founded the Patowmack Company, which built skirting canals to make the Potomac River navigable, and kept up with the company's progress during his two-term presidency. James Madison visited the former president after his retirement to Mount Vernon and reported that the zeal with which Washington still supported the blasting of canal channels was so intense as hardly to be described.

In the late 18th century, proponents began surveying canal routes and in 1808, Albert Gallatin, Secretary of the Treasury, recommended that federal funds be used to build several canals as part of a comprehensive effort to develop transportation routes. Many canals were underway or about to move off the drawing boards when the War of 1812 diverted the country's attention and resources.

Despite this early activity, the Erie Canal was still an extraordinarily bold undertaking. Thomas Jefferson called it a splendid project in 1809, adding, "it is little short of madness to think of it at this time." By 1816, only 100 miles of canals had been built in the entire country and the longest canal extended less than 30 miles. The Erie, which was authorized by the state legislature in 1817, eventually stretched 363 miles from the Hudson River to Lake Erie, crossing the Appalachian Mountains to reach its destination.

The cost of the canal was projected at $6 million. Federal support was out of the question after James Madison vetoed the Bonus Bill that would have provided funds to states for internal improvements. The price tag alone should have deterred even the most determined optimist, since New York State had a population of only about a million and a half people, most of whom were scraping out a living as farmers.

Only a handful of the country's small group of engineers had any experience building canals. They learned their trade by traveling to Great Britain or Europe and studying systems already in place. Nothing remotely like a skilled labor force was available for the actual construction, which would pass through long stretches of unpopulated wilderness. The enterprise turned out to be a gigantic experiment in on-the-job training.

Improbably, however, Clinton's gamble paid off with a spectacular success. Canal sections opened as soon as they were completed. By 1824, $300,000 in tolls had been collected and in 1826, when the entire canal route officially opened, that figure more than doubled. The canal had earned nearly $125 million by 1882, when tolls were abolished.

The cost of transporting goods fell dramatically, while commercial opportunities exploded. Nathaniel Hawthorne captured this transformation in a story in which he says the water of the canal "causes towns—with their masses of brick and stone, their churches and theaters, their business and hubbub, their luxury and refinement, their gay dames and polished citizens—to spring up." New York became the country's principal seaport and villages like Rochester, Schenectady and Utica turned into small cities.

Leaders in nearby states feared that New York's prosperity might come at the expense of their constituents and they set about building canals that would offer alternative transportation routes. Politicians, speculators and businessmen everywhere were dazzled by the rewards brought by the Erie Canal and hoped for similar financial bonanzas. Canal building exploded, particularly in the Mid-Atlantic area. By the end of the canal era, Pennsylvania alone had more than 1,200 miles of canals, about one-quarter of the total built throughout the country.

The period of intense canal-building activity was relatively short. A financial panic in 1837 turned into a severe depression, threatening existing projects and increasing the risk of new commitments. In state after state, railroads began to challenge canals for control over the transport of goods. About six thousand miles were added to the railroad system in the 1840s, a total larger than all the canal miles ever built.

The audacity it took to build the Erie Canal turned into recklessness in the waning days of the canal era. The state legislature in Indiana, for example, voted for an ambitious system of state canals in 1836 and by 1841, had run up a debt of over $13 million. That state also lost $2.5 million, which had been invested in the company that built the Morris Canal in New Jersey. By 1839, Pennsylvania had a state debt of $32 million, most of which was attributable to its canal-building efforts. Less than 20 years later, its mammoth system of public works was up for sale.

THE CANAL RESTORATION MOVEMENT

Less than one hundred years after the Erie Canal's spectacular opening, vegetation and debris obliterated towpaths; historic structures crumbled and canal beds went dry. By 1925, only 700 miles of canals in the United States were in use.

Stories of how these waterways came into being were also vanishing. A few books offered descriptions of the canal era, but their tone was often wistful, even defensive. The most eloquent of these early chroniclers, Alvin Harlow, wrote, "The history of our canals is a significant commentary upon American life and character—restless as it is, eager for speed, yearning to change, tearing down as soon as we have built."

Fast forward about 70 years to a hotel in downtown Providence, Rhode Island. Participants at the World Canal Conference in 1997 fill the main dining room, where they hear greetings from local officials eager to tout the region's waterways. During the next three days, canal buffs, historians, park managers and tourism promoters board early-morning buses for tours of historic sites. The sophisticated display of the region's attractions is the work of the Blackstone Valley Tourism Council, which labored for nearly a year on the event.

Lobbying is so intense for the chance to host subsequent

conferences that the board of directors appoints a special committee to select sites. Its members come up with a list—Illinois, France, New York, Ireland and Montreal—that diplomatically alternates North American and European locations. "It's a big change from what happened six years ago," says Dave Johnson. "The last day of the conference someone pointed at us and said 'let's go to the C&O Canal next year.' They probably made the decision in the bar the night before."

After years of neglect, canals have become a favorite tool for promoting economic development. Advocates point first to Lowell, Massachusetts. Life was hard for its residents, after its textile mills closed. But in 1978, designation of the Lowell National Historic Park spurred an economic transformation. The park, which includes a restored section of the Pawtucket Canal, preserves and interprets the history of the Industrial Revolution. For every one dollar of public investment an estimated seven dollars has been pumped into the local economy.

According to Jim Amon, executive director of the Delaware and Raritan Canal Commission, proximity to the New Jersey canal park raises the value of homes and attracts business to the area. He adds, "Many New Jersey residents vacation near the canal, instead of leaving the state."

The National Canal Museum, which shares a site with the Crayola Factory in downtown Easton, Pa., had resulted in 100 new businesses and business expansions only a year after its opening. At the western end of the Chesapeake and Ohio Canal in Cumberland, Md., the Canal Place Authority is working with a package of more than $45 million in federal and state funds for projects that will attract tourists interested in transportation history.

The federal government is giving a powerful push to these developments through its national heritage program. Congressionally designated national heritage areas are eligible for up to $1 million in federal funds annually for 10 years on a 50-50 cost-sharing basis. Technical assistance and management support are also provided.

In 1984, the Illinois and Michigan Canal Corridor

became the country's first national heritage area. The
Blackstone River Valley National Heritage Corridor, which
encompasses the Blackstone Canal, received designation in
1986. Two years later, Congress designated the Delaware
and Lehigh Navigation Canal Corridor and in 1996, added
the Ohio and Erie Canal National Heritage Corridor.

Designation has become a hotly contested prize.
Beginning in 1989, the Ohio and Erie Canal Corridor
Coalition spent several years talking with anyone who
would listen about their plans and hopes. Congressman
Ralph Regula battled to get funds for a National Park
Service study in 1990 to determine the feasibility of a canal
heritage corridor.

The opening of the Cuyahoga Valley National
Recreation Area Towpath Trail in 1993 gave residents an
idea of what the heritage corridor could offer and business
leaders began to see the project in terms of benefits for their
employees. The NPS study found that the area was suffi-
ciently historical to receive designation. In 1994, the House
of Representatives passed the necessary legislation, but the
bill was killed by the Senate. Finally, in August 1996, both
congressional chambers passed the legislation, which was
signed by President Clinton in November.

What brought about this 20th-century version of canal
mania? Head for a canal park to discover the simple answer
to this question. The area offers something for just about
everyone. For a city-dweller, it's a stretch of greenery—usually with the added bonus of peacefully flowing water.
Visitors can hike, bike, stroll and sometimes, ski down the
towpath. Add a museum or a canal boat for a wonderful
lesson in 19th-century history.

The more complicated answer is that a few individuals
and voluntary organizations devoted themselves to preserv-
ing canals and their history until the rest of the country
caught up with them. This hard-working group of enthusi-
asts includes amateur historians, engineers, environmentalists, community activists, naturalists and others who didn't
want to wait around for tourism departments to discover the
treasures in their backyards.

You'll find some of their stories throughout this book. Jim Lee, for example, was a railroad conductor who spent hours talking to Morris Canal boatmen as a teenager. He later bought and restored a planetender's house, amassed a collection of memorabilia and published several books about the canal, including *Tales the Boatmen Told*. Lee shared his interests with Hugh Moore, a passenger on his route, who eventually purchased land for one of the country's first canal parks.

William Shank, an engineer whose ties to canal life go back four generations, researched and wrote *The Amazing Pennsylvania Canals*, at a time when most historians treated the canal era only as a brief precursor to the more famous period of western expansion by rail. In 1948, as a young navy ensign stationed in Washington, D.C., Tom Hahn began exploring the area around the C&O Canal and later published a mile-by-mile guide to the towpath, now in its 14th edition.

The canal restoration movement owes a huge debt to the members of the American Canal Society. Hahn, Shank and William Trout founded the organization in 1972, shortly after the successful battle to enact federal legislation creating the Chesapeake and Ohio Canal National Historical Park. That struggle convinced Hahn that a national organization was needed to "represent the interests of all Americans concerning the preservation and restoration of the canals of the United States."

In short order, representatives of eight state canal societies joined the organization's board, 200 individuals signed up as members and a journal, *American Canals*, was launched. The second edition of the journal contained this modest proposal: "Get communities to restore sections. At least clear out saplings etc. and provide a path alongside. Restoration of locks for historical value." The society began a canal index and a list of restored areas.

The society has fulfilled Hahn's hopes that it could serve as a clearinghouse for information and stimulate restoration projects. In an issue of *American Canals* commemorating the society's 20th anniversary, Shank writes that the organization has grown "to an international organization of 860 members, whose advice and counsel is sought by individual canal researchers and historical agencies worldwide."

Most of the real work is done through state canal societies, where activities range from the glamourous to the gritty. In 1998, a canal restoration project headed by members of the C&O Canal Association ended up as national news. Hillary Rodham Clinton announced that the Monocacy Aqueduct had been placed on the National Trust for Historic Preservation's list of America's most endangered historic places.

Canal society members sponsor cleanup days, restore historic artifacts, organize trips, produce publications, serve as museum docents, plan festivals and lobby for public funds. Try out one of the events and you'll discover a good mixture of hard-core canal aficionados who want to share their lore and newcomers who are eager to hear it.

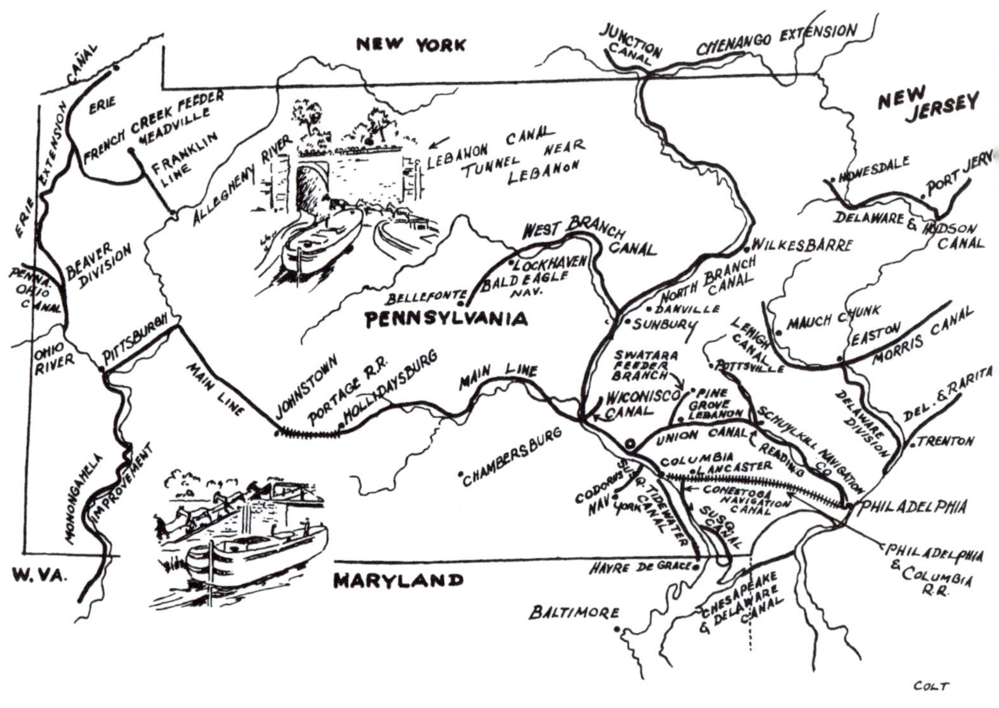

With more than 1,200 miles of canals, Pennsylvania's canal system was called one of the wonders of the western world.

PENNSYLVANIA

First, most, longest, Pennsylvania's canal history is filled with superlatives. Nearly 100 years before the Revolutionary War, William Penn proposed a canal between the Susquehanna and Schuylkill Rivers to link Philadelphia with western Pennsylvania. In 1762, engineers conducted the first canal survey in the United States along that route, mapping out the course for what later became the Union Canal.

Geographic obstacles, such as the Allegheny Mountains and the rapids of the Lehigh River, were merely problems to be overcome. They served to unleash a marvelous display of engineering ingenuity and good old American persistence. *Do whatever it takes to get there*—that was the mood of the state's most energetic leaders and entrepreneurs.

Those pragmatic canal builders designed two ingenious rail systems, the Allegheny Portage Railroad and Switchback Railroad, to complement and extend canal transportation and also constructed the country's first railroad tunnel, first double-track railroad and first cable suspension bridge. The Mainline Canal, which stretched 395 miles from Philadelphia to Pittsburgh, combined rail, river and canal transportation.

By the end of the canal craze, Pennsylvania had more than 1,200 miles of canals. Historian Thomas Cochran called the state's canal system one of the wonders of the western world, adding, "except for France, no nation in history had ever equaled Pennsylvania's improvement of water transportation within such a brief period, and French construction was easier."

The state claimed the longest and most expensive publicly

funded canal system, but it also was home to Josiah White, one of the era's most energetic canal entrepreneurs. This combination of public and private ownership produced a time of relentless canal-building activity that lasted until the mid-19th century.

All that activity carried a price tag. Before the canal fever broke, Pennsylvania legislators had accumulated the largest debt for internal improvements of any state in the country. By 1840, Pennsylvania owed $40 million, $2 million of which went to pay interest on the debt. To make the situation even more unsavory, much of the money was due to the British. A 5-year period of economic recession resulted in a default on the interest payments in 1841 and 1842, although the entire amount eventually was paid.

Historians and others frequently play what-should-have-been about Pennsylvania's expensive canal-building era. Thomas Cochran observed, "Perhaps never in history has such a great man-made transport system had so short a useful life." The frantic effort to build canals quickly was followed by an even more frenetic period of railroad construction.

That initial explosion of canal-building activity left important legacies, however. It promoted westward expansion, the growth of the coal industry and served to legitimize the use of public funds and powers to promote economic development.

Get a copy of William Shank's book, *The Amazing Pennsylvania Canals*, for historic descriptions of all the state's canals. Many of them can be seen only in old pictures or one's own imagination. But there's still a wonderfully varied collection of canal-related sites to visit. A short drive from the high-tech displays at the National Canal Museum at Easton is a lovingly restored lockhouse and park in the very small canal town of Freemansburg.

To appreciate the engineering triumphs of the period, visit the Allegheny Portage Railroad National Historic Site or go to Jim Thorpe for a look at a working model of the Switchback Railroad. The canal era's human history is represented at such sites as Eckley Miners' Village and re-created at canal festivals. Better yet, head for the Delaware Canal and hike or bike along the country's last remaining continuously watered towpath canal.

Here are the legacies of Pennsylvania's canal-building era. They are grouped geographically, beginning with the Delaware and Lehigh Navigation Canal National Heritage Corridor at the eastern part of the state, moving to the Allegheny Mountain area of central Pennsylvania and ending with sites scattered about the state.

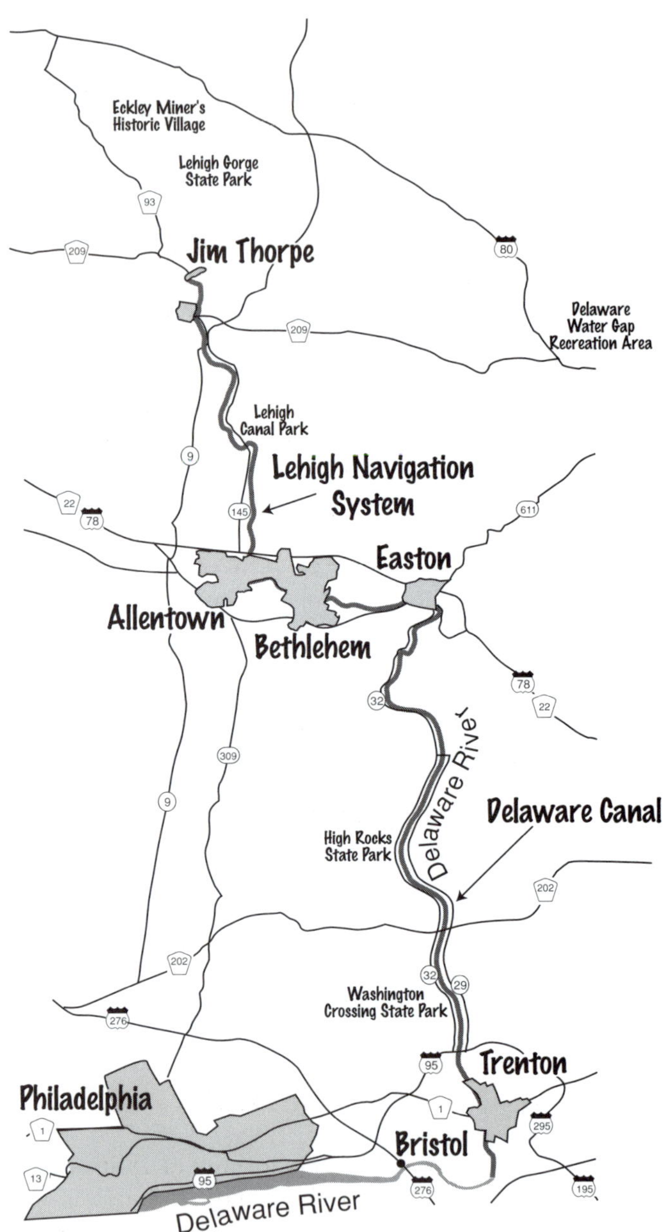

Nearly every facet of canal history can be found somewhere along this 150-mile stretch of land, which follows the routes of the Delaware Canal from Bristol to Easton and the Lehigh Navigation System from Easton to Wilkes Barre. It was designated the Delaware and Lehigh Navigation Canal National Heritage Corridor in 1988.

Delaware and Lehigh Navigation Canal National Heritage Corridor

The long name results from a new federal approach to parks. Rather than buying up extensive tracts of land, the federal government is targeting technical and financial assistance to historic and culturally significant areas with the aim of stimulating state, local and private revitalization efforts. The canal navigation system was deemed the unifying theme of this 150-mile strip of land, which Congress designated a heritage corridor in 1988.

You won't find a uniformly well-maintained park or towpath trail. In fact, the heritage corridor offers a visual reminder of the challenges of canal restoration, as well as its rewards. Some areas are virtually unwalkable—marred by debris and overgrown vegetation—and have limited or no access to a canal or other attractions. Others are beautifully maintained, with interpretive displays, ample recreational opportunities and convenient entry points.

The heritage corridor literally is a work in progress. In 1996, National Park Service staff issued a plan to guide development of a 112-mile Delaware and Lehigh Trail along the corridor. The document describes specific steps to reclaim the 70 miles of the trail that were unprotected. (See Resources.)

National Canal Museum

Canal history became big business in June of 1996, when dignitaries gathered to cut a ribbon to open the new National Canal Museum in downtown Easton. A more appropriate ceremony followed inside the building, when 62 small containers of water from canals from all over the world were poured together in an oak cask. The "Wedding of the Waters" symbolized the partnership among canals necessary to create an inland waterway.

The museum shares a central location (and an admission fee) with an unlikely neighbor. For the price of $7, visitors can tour the museum and The Crayola Factory, which are part of an ambitious effort to recast Easton as a tourist destination. A visitor's center for the heritage corridor is also housed in the Two Rivers Landing complex.

For many years, the state budget included authorization for funds to build a museum that would enhance the resources of an existing canal museum in Hugh Moore Park. But funds never were appropriated until a broad range of interests converged to produce a powerful partnership.

The key corporate partner in the new public-private partnership is Binney & Smith, makers of Crayola crayons. The company had been deluged with requests from parents and teachers for kid-friendly factory tours. Their solution was The Crayola Factory, a learning center created specifically for children, who can watch crayons being made, draw on walls and floors, and participate in computer-generated projects.

The public members of the coalition were also hard at work developing support for the new museum and the Two Rivers Landing complex. Stephen Humphrey, executive director of the museum, says, "We had a three-inch-thick binder containing letters of support to show to the governor. The project became a five-county effort, with our plans to package the area as a multi-day tourist destination."

Funds eventually came from the federal Community Development Block Grant program, the state, city, Hugh Moore Trust and hundreds of individuals and small organizations. The names of donors are carved in Vermont granite stone on the walkway in front of the complex.

"You have turned the corner," said Department of Interior representative Kenneth Smith, at the opening ceremony. "This city has the look and feel of being prosperous."

Another official was looking ahead to a first-year attendance of 300,000 and projecting 600,000 visitors annually in the future. Humphrey estimated that at the end of 1998, 100 new businesses and business expansions had resulted from the new complex.

Nancy Dunna-
vant pours water
from the Dismal
Swamp Canal
into an oak cask
for Wedding of
Waters ceremony.

The canal-crayon combination works surprisingly well. Visitors enter a comfortable auditorium on the ground floor for an introductory video. The shift from crayons to canal history in the film's narrative can be jarring, but both attractions get their due. You can make a quick retreat from the noise of the school groups by taking an elevator directly to the canal museum on the third floor.

The museum is small, but makes good use of its space. A video offers an excellent introductory synopsis of canal history, which includes a sympathetic portrayal of canal workers. Exhibits are simple and use technology to elucidate, rather than to dazzle. Look for the map that traces the history of American canal building. Flashing lights illuminate the paths of canals as they are described by a narrator. Operating models of an inclined plane and a lock show how these famous canal engineering features work. The museum also contains displays about canal-related occupations, mules and family life on canal boats.

Exhibits are geared to casual visitors and children. The museum is not yet a place to explore the complicated economic and historical issues that are a part of this fascinating era, but staff are adding new material. The building's fourth floor will be devoted to a changing series of exhibits and a permanent display on modern canals will open on the third floor.

The Pennsylvania Canal Society remains actively involved with the operation of the museum, which displays many items on loan from the organization. Members serve as docents at the museum and develop lectures on transportation history offered in the museum's auditorium.

Two blocks south of U.S. 22 or 1.5 miles north of the Easton exit of I-78. Open year-round. Admission. 30 Centre Square, Easton 18042. 610-559-6613.

Hugh Moore Historical Park

Hugh Moore, creator of the Dixie cup, was a farsighted businessman, who backed such causes as the United Nations. He also recognized the importance of green space and donated $300,000 to the city of Easton to purchase park land along the lower six miles of the Lehigh River. In 1966, Moore and others developed a master plan for the new canal park that anticipates the recent discovery that historic preservation can be good business.

They wrote, "Our proposals embody numerous suggestions to develop and heighten the awareness of this historic evolution evolving around the economic factors and growth of transportation of the Valley over the past 216 years. Although we envision a park which should make living on its shores more attractive, it is expected to be of economic value as well."

The first canal museum opened in 1970 at the Forks of the Delaware as a cooperative effort between Easton's Hugh Moore Park Commission and the Pennsylvania Canal Society. The Junior League of Lehigh Valley helped research the interior exhibits of the Locktender's House Museum, which opened in 1974. Four years later, the Friends of the Hugh Moore Park bought the canal boat *Josiah White*. A full-time historian joined the staff in 1980 and redesigned exhibits to reflect the national experience with the towpath canal era.

Look up at the cables of the Chain Bridge, which span the Lehigh River between the park and the river's south shore. They were manufactured by the Lehigh Coal and Navigation's pioneering wire rope factory at what is now the town of Jim Thorpe and was then named Mauch Chunk. The factory was the first in the United States to produce machine-made wire rope, and the cables of the Change Bridge are its oldest existing products.

The Locktender's House Museum presents the life of a locktender and his family, through a series of period rooms and a costumed interpreter. The Abbott Street Industrial Area was the most important early industrial area in South Easton and between 1830 and 1850 was one of Easton's first industrial parks. It had a sawmill, grist mill, and cotton mill.

Island Park is one of the most beautiful and historically significant areas in the park. Its approximately 100 acres of land area are located in the slackwater pool formed by the Lehigh Navigation's Chain Dam. A large scale ice cutting and storage industry developed on the island. Later, it was home to an amusement park, featuring mechanical rides and a carousel, and today, is a wildlife sanctuary.

From U.S. 22, take 25th Street south to Lehigh Drive, turn right, go .5 miles to stop sign and turn right at entrance bridge to park. Admission for canal boat ride. 200 S. Delaware St., Easton 18044. 610-515-8000.

Easton

Three canals met near Easton during the 19th century. The Lehigh Canal flowed south to join the Delaware Canal. A cable ferry carried canal boats across the Delaware River to nearby Phillipsburg in New Jersey, where canal boats could enter the Morris Canal and eventually unload their cargo in Newark.

Five major railroads also served the area, resulting in an early industrial center, linking New York, Philadelphia and the anthracite coal regions. Even earlier, Easton had the distinction of being one of only three colonial cities in which the Declaration of Independence was read to a public audience.

The recent expansion and relocation of the National Canal Museum have given the entire town an economic boost and a chance to show off its attractions to a new audience. During the tourist season, trolley tours connect the Two Rivers Landing complex, which houses the museum and Crayola exhibits, with the canal boat ride at Hugh Moore Park.

Easton is also a terrific city to explore on foot. Centre Square is the focal point of the downtown area and the site of the famous reading of the Declaration of Independence. In the 18th century, Indian treaty councils were held there, before the British conquest of the Ohio Valley during the French and Indian Wars.

Today, the restaurants and stores around the square offer an intriguing glimpse of a small town in transition. Easton Sweet Shop, open since 1922, is a small-town diner. Elvis Presley is on the juke box, and the booths are upholstered in red vinyl. On one wall are posters of Marilyn

*Easton's famous
Centre Square*

Monroe and James Dean and on the other is a mural showing the restaurant in its early days. It hasn't changed much.

Walk a few 100 feet to Pearly Baker's Ale House. You'll
feel as if you've stepped into a trendy restaurant that could
fit into the gentrified area of any major American city. Don't
miss the Quadrant Book Mart & Coffee House at 20 N.
Third St., less than a block from the square. It's an old
house, with books lining the walls and tilting precariously
on tables and the floor. The pastry is wonderful and the
owners will leave you alone to browse.

The buildings bordering the square are a wonderful mix
of 18th- and 19th-century architectural styles, including
Victorian, Beaux Arts and Art Deco. Walk one block over
to Northhampton Street for examples of Easton's 19th-cen-
tury commercial buildings and the Easton House Tavern,
which was frequented by Benjamin Franklin and George

Washington. Take a short walk to Fourth Street, where the Northampton County Historical and Genealogical Society is home to displays of paintings, furniture, tools, chinaware, dolls, and jewelry dating from pre-colonial times to the present.

From Philadelphia and South Jersey. Take 611 north to downtown Easton or take the northeast extension of the Pennsylvania Turnpike to exit #33. Exit at 4th Street. 610-515-1200. www.easton-pa.org.

Delaware Canal State Park

The Delaware Canal, which runs 60 miles from Bristol to Easton, was plagued with problems during its construction. Famed canal-builder Josiah White, who was called in to save the state-funded project, made a blunt assessment of his predecessors' work: "You have used poor materials, poor workmanship... it will not hold water. The canal is a moist ditch."

White had earned a right to his harsh judgment. The Delaware Canal had been authorized by the state legislature in 1827 for completion in 1829, but was not fully operational until 1832. White and his partners started work on the slack water and canal navigation system from Mauch Chunk to Easton at about the same time and finished in less than two years. They were waiting anxiously for the connecting link that would allow their coal-filled canal boats access to markets in Philadelphia and New York.

Nothing could detract from the canal's advantageous location, however. Boats could reach New York via the Morris Canal at Phillipsburg, New Jersey and the Delaware & Raritan Canal at Lambertville. The canal became the only consistently profitable segment of the Pennsylvania State Canal System.

The park owes its existence to one of the country's first canal associations, a group founded in 1932, and is protected by a successor to that organization, whose members began by picking up trash and painting bridges and ended up with a First Prize in the Take Pride in America award of 1990.

Canal preservation efforts began immediately after the last boat traveled north along the canal. The Delaware Valley Protective Association was formed in 1932 to protect a section of the canal at New Hope and for four years, ran a converted scow along a seven-mile stretch of canal. Members collected 80,000 signatures to get part of the canal area designated the Theodore Roosevelt State Park in 1940.

The outcome was worth all that energy and organizing. The Delaware Canal, watered for its 60-mile length, is the only remaining continuously intact reminder of the towpath canal-building era. It offers wonderful hiking, biking, bird-watching and canoeing opportunities.

An incredible array of attractions can be found in or near the park. The art galleries, antique shops, restaurants and cultural resources of New Hope are nationally famous, but you'll be sharing them with other people, lots of other people. The town draws one million sightseers and shoppers annually. For canal fans, the major attractions are the New Hope Mule Barge, which takes visitors five miles up the canal to a picnic stop and the restored lockhouse that serves as headquarters for the Friends of the Delaware Canal, the contemporary successor to the Delaware Valley Protective Association.

Lumberville, Point Pleasant and Uhlerstown are canal villages that have not yet been transformed by tourism. Washington's Crossing State Park commemorates one of the most important battles of the Revolutionary War, while Pennsybury Manor was the home of one of the country's first canal advocates: William Penn. In Bristol, volunteers from area unions excavated and restored a beautiful canal lagoon. It had previously been filled in to build a skating rink.

There are numerous entry points to the park. The Locktender's House is at 145 South Main St., New Hope 18938. 215-862-2021. The canal barge landing is at 149 South Main St. 215-862-0758. Fee for boat trip.

Three Stubborn Women

Betty Orlemann says, "My husband and I used to sit on our outside deck, waving to people who canoed past on the Delaware Canal." The view was not always idyllic, however. Orlemann, who moved to Smithtown in 1977, remembers that the canal would run out of water or suffer flood damage. The towpath was in poor condition.

Orlemann took her concerns to the park superintendent and anyone else who would listen. Florence Schaffhausen, a columnist from the *Doylestown Intelligencer* offered some advice. "Just do it," she said, when Orlemann worried aloud that she didn't know how to start an organization.

Thirty people showed up for the first meeting in 1982 at the Towpath House restaurant in New Hope, including a handful who had been members of the Delaware Valley Protective Association, which had pressured the state into turning the canal area into a park. Members of the new organization, Friends of the Delaware Canal, got to work on projects that had a quick and visible payoff. They painted bridges, repaired stone walls and cleaned debris from the canal's water and towpath.

Orlemann made certain the public and elected officials knew about all that activity. The organization received newspaper, radio and television publicity and soon had the support of federal and state representatives and the director of the Bureau of State Parks. Friends led guided walking tours on the towpath, hiking about 12 miles each Saturday for five consecutive weeks. They developed a canal show with slides and an old canal movie, which was narrated by two former boatmen, Howard and Frank Swope, and shown at schools.

Board member Zabel Davis led one of the most ambitious efforts. The park superintendent said that a dredge was desperately needed to dig up silt in the canal. When the price tag for such a machine was deemed too high for the state, Davis mounted a three-year long Pledge for the Dredge Campaign.

Members worked at the grass-roots level: holding teas and barge parties, collecting spare change in store canisters and selling a cookbook. But they also went after larger donations from businesses and local governments. At the christening of the dredge, named the *Zabel Belle*, the Director of State Parks said the $100,000 gift was the most money raised by an organization for a state project.

The Friends then persuaded the state to buy a canal lockhouse at New Hope and hired an executive director, Susan Taylor, to make sure the organization could satisfy its end of the bargain: restoring the historic structure and creating a museum.

Taylor, who had been active in municipal government, knew how to unearth funding sources. She and others persuaded the Pew Charitable Trust to make a challenge grant, matched with funds from the newly created heritage corridor. The total of $60,000 was enough to get the project underway. In 1996, the completed project won the Preservation Award from the Preservation Alliance for Greater Philadelphia and an architectural award from the Bucks County Chapter of the American Institute of Architects.

Lehigh Canal
and Navigation System

This transportation route, which runs 72 miles from White Haven in the upper Lehigh River Valley to Easton, is very different from the straightforward Delaware Canal. The term navigation system was used because Josiah White, the entrepreneurial genius behind the Lehigh Coal and Navigation Company, needed a combination of engineering methods and transportation devices to get coal from the Allegheny Mountains to Easton and ultimately, to Philadelphia. The system included America's first coal railroad, river dams of unprecedented size, a railroad powered primarily by the force of gravity, as well as the Lehigh Canal.

This section of the heritage corridor is a work in progress, when contrasted with the well-maintained Delaware Canal State Park. Take a look at the *D&L Trail Workbook* (see Resources) to learn about restoration plans. Currently, a 20-mile biking and hiking trail along the route of the Lehigh Canal links Easton with Bethlehem and Allentown. Trexler Park in Allentown is the heart of an attractive urban park system.

One of three remaining lockhouses on the Lehigh Canal

Bethlehem is renowned as the home of Bethlehem Steel, and it was also the site of an 18th-century Moravian settlement.

The small canal town of Freemansburg is one of the highlights of the trail. Members of the Old Freemansburg Association restored Lockhouse #44, one of three remaining original lockhouses on the Lehigh Canal. The property also contains the remains of a mule barn, locks, grist mill and bridge. The association sponsors a monthly guided canal hike, lectures, trips to other historic sites and Old Market Days, a two-day festival of arts and crafts.

Further west, members of the Walnutport Canal Association bought a stone locktender's house in 1985 and began a multi-year restoration project, which includes an effort to collect period furnishings. The association has also raised more than $100,000 to restore the lock.

From I-78, take the Hellerton exit and go north on 412 toward Bethlehem. After the second railroad overpass, bear right to follow the sign toward Freemansburg. Go left across the Lehigh River bridge and continue on Main Street to the end of town. Bear right on Lockhouse Road. Open on Sundays from 1:00 to 4:00, May through October.

From Allentown take Route 145 north 13 miles to Walnutport, turn left at traffic light on Main St and travel one block south to the lockhouse.

An Early Entrepreneur

Neither fire nor flood stopped Josiah White's drive to develop the Lehigh Valley, but the Pennsylvania canal builder had no interest in the luxuries of wealth. His customary apparel was a red flannel shirt, buckskin paints tanned in oil to resist water and boots of his own invention. Holes cut in the toes let out the water as White worked in the Lehigh River.

White had already bought and turned around a failed hardware store, before he was 21. The young entrepreneur's journal records his ambition "to have enough at 30 and to work thereafter for God and my brothers." White calculated that he would need $40,000, so that he could invest half of the funds and live off the interest.

That goal accomplished, White bought land with the aim of developing water power at the falls of the Schuylkill River and built a number of mills along the river to manufacture the new wire products that he had dreamed up in his effort to channel the power of the falls. A fire destroyed his mills, but the newly impoverished entrepreneur rebuilt his business.

White turned his attention to the commercial possibilities of bringing anthracite coal from eastern Pennsylvania down the Lehigh River. He and his partner Erskine Hazard agreed to give one ear of corn each year to the Lehigh Coal Mine Company, pay property taxes and ship 40,000 bushels of coal to Philadelphia, three years after signing a contract that gave them a 21-year lease on coal lands. In 1818, the state legislature approved the document, which granted the two men the right to develop the Lehigh River for navigation, saying, "Gentlemen, you have our permission to ruin yourselves."

The partners set up camp at Mauch Chunk, hired more than 500 men and began building dams in the treacherous river waters."I was in the water with them most of the time," White said later. "I didn't know anything about blasting nor did they. But we were lucky; as I recollect we lost only two men."

When the conventional dam of the day proved inadequate, White invented a new dam and lock system, the Bear Trap Lock, which produced an artificial flood that floated the coal-carrying arks from one dam to the next. It should come as no surprise that the two men met their deadline with time to spare.

At first, navigation was downstream only. Arks constructed near Mauch Chunk were broken up in Philadelphia, where the lumber was sold. The boatmen walked or rode back to Mauch Chunk for the next journey down the Lehigh River. In 1825, White decided to build a canal up the river from Easton to Mauch Chunk, which would permit two-way navigation.

White went on to extend the navigable water 26 miles from Mauch Chunk to the coal-producing area of White Haven by a combination slackwater and canal system. The job required huge locks to permit passage along a particularly tumultuous stretch of the Lehigh River and had an estimated price tag of over $1 million. After a site visit of the completed project, the state's canal commissioners wrote, "We were filled with admiration and delight when we examined these stupendous works, which have made the Lehigh from a shallow, wild useless stream into a calm and beautiful river."

White's story is more than an engaging rags-to-riches-to-rags-to-riches tale. The Philadelphia Quaker was acting on a strong set of religious values, when he built the Lehigh Coal and Navigation Company. He ate with his servants and offered medical care and education to his workers. Personal tragedies—the death of his first wife and three sons—brought deep pain, but they never thwarted his determination to develop the Lehigh Valley.

"Our manufactured goods are a mere trifle, compared to what is imported," wrote White. He argued that the development of American commercial enterprises was necessary to decrease dependence on Great Britain, and transportation routes were key to that development. The indefatigable entrepreneur met each new obstacle with an almost miraculous display of persistence and ingenuity. He was determined to do his part to build a new country.

Jim Thorpe-Mauch Chunk

As Jim Thorpe, this town is a popular tourist destination with historic B&Bs, stunning scenery, mountain biking and art galleries. But for canal fans, its greatest charms lie in its links to the past, when it was called Mauch Chunk and served as the center of Josiah White's mining and transportation empire.

The Switchback Railroad brought coal from Summit Hill to Mauch Chunk, where it was loaded on boats for the trip down the Lehigh Canal. The force of gravity brought rail cars loaded with coal and mules nine miles down to the foot of the hill, where the animals disembarked and then dragged the empty cars back up the hill. (With typical White efficiency, the mules were fed on the downward journey.)

White and his partners later built engine houses with stationary steam engines at the top of Mt. Pisgah and Mt. Jefferson and a series of inclined planes up the eastern slope of Mt. Pisgah. A Barney car powered by a steam engine pushed empty rail cars up the inclines, and rail traffic flowed in a continuous loop.

The Switchback Railroad had a second career and longer life as a tourist attraction. For nearly 60 years, people paid to be frightened out of their wits as they dropped down the steep mountain in so-called pleasure cars. That spectacle inspired the invention of the world's first roller coaster. Named the Switchback Railroad, it opened at Coney Island in 1884.

Visit the Mauch Chunk Museum and Cultural Center to see a working model of that famous train and pick up a brochure that describes walking and driving tours that trace the rail journey. The track itself was dismantled and sold for scrap metal.

Local businessman Asa Packer personified the shift from canals to railroads. He operated coal boats on the Lehigh Canal, made his first fortune as a boat builder, and in 1851 gained control of the Lehigh Valley Railroad, the canal's chief rival. The former canal boat captain built a rail line from Mauch Chunk to Easton, the same route he had traveled on the water as a young man. When Packer died in 1879, his railroad encompassed 650 miles of track from New York to the New Jersey seaboard and his estate was valued at $54 million.

The Asa Packer Mansion shows the rewards of the transportation revolution for one family. An observatory

tops the ornate four-story Victorian structure, which is a
short walk from the historic downtown area. Inside are the
accouterments of 19th-century wealth: gold-embroidered
draperies, a solid ebony Steinway piano, hand-carved
mahogany paneling and a crystal chandelier so dazzling that
it was copied for the movie *Gone with the Wind.*

Here's the story of the town's name change, although
there's not a canal in it. Jim Thorpe was a two-time
Olympic medalist, who suffered discrimination because of
his Native American ancestry. His widow resolved to find a
way of honoring him after his death. She and her representatives persuaded local officials that if they changed the
town's name and provided the dead athlete with a suitable
memorial, a museum, hospital and even the National
Football Hall of Fame might be located in the newly named
town of Jim Thorpe. The grand plans fell through, but the
town lived up to its side of the bargain.

As Jim Thorpe, the town is becoming a tourist destination once again. The old Mauch Chunk Opera House
reopened as a performing arts center. A wedding gift from
Asa Packer to his son Harry is now an elegant bed and
breakfast, which hosts Victorian balls. Galleries, gift shops
and restaurants line the narrow streets of the downtown
area. Perhaps the strangest development is the metamorpho-
sis of an abandoned Presbyterian church into the Josiah
White Exhibition Center for Contemporary Art. It's hard to
imagine what that austere Quaker would think of this effort
to pay him homage.

*From Philadelphia or the Scranton-Wilkes-Barre area, take the
Northeast Extension of the Pennsylvania Turnpike (Rt. 9).From
exit 34, follow U.S. 209 south through Lehighton to Jim Thorpe.
The visitor's center is housed in the Jersey Central Passenger
Station in downtown Jim Thorpe at the corner of Asa Packer
Park and Route 209.*

Lehigh Gorge State Park

This ruggedly scenic park boasts attractions, even for visitors who are unaware of its canal and railroad history.
Lehigh River offers gorgeous waterfalls, opportunities for

Class III whitewater rafting and tamer boating experiences. One of the state's most beautiful rail-trails follows the abandoned railroad grade of the Central Railroad of New Jersey. During the winter, 15 miles of the trail are open for cross-country skiing and snowmobiling.

The park also provides visitors a chance to put themselves in Josiah White's boots, when he struggled to get coal and lumber down the Pennsylvania mountains to Mauch Chunk for its trip on the Lehigh Canal. He constructed 20 dams and 29 locks over the 26 miles of the Lehigh River between Mauch Chunk and White Haven, overcoming an elevation change of about 600 feet. Less than five miles of the final system consisted of canal navigation. The system was destroyed by flooding in 1862, but remains of the locks, dams and towpath are still visible and interpretive kiosks explain the area's history. They are located at the three main access points: White Haven, Rockport and Glen Onoko.

To Rockport, the central area and location of the park ranger station, follow 209 south from Jim Thorpe to Route 93 north, continue to S.R. 2055 (Lehigh Gorge Drive), through Weatherly to Rockport at S.R. 4014. 888-PA-PARKS. www. dcnr.state.pa.us/stateparks/parks

Eckley Miner's Village

Visit this very small town (20 inhabitants) to get an idea of what life was like for the miners who dug the coal that eventually floated down the Lehigh Canal. The visitor's center offers videos, exhibits on life in mining towns and a walking tour that encompasses 23 historic sites and structures.

Eckley is a curious mix of an actual mining village and a Hollywood version of the same thing. Most of the shooting for the movie "The Molly Maguires" took place here. The producers used existing buildings and built a company store, which is still standing. They also constructed what is now the largest structure in town: a replica of a building known as a breaker, where coal was processed

After the filming, a non-profit corporation raised $100,000 to buy the town from its owner and then donated the village to the state. With $2.4 million in state funds, staff have embarked on an ambitious project to restore the homes and use them to tell the story of 19th-century class relationships.

From White Haven, turn left onto route 940. Go 6 miles to Freeland; turn left at Auto Exchange and go 3 miles. Admission. RR#2, Box 236, Weatherly 18255. 717-636-2070.

Mining town meets Hollywood: much of "The Molly Maguires" was filmed here

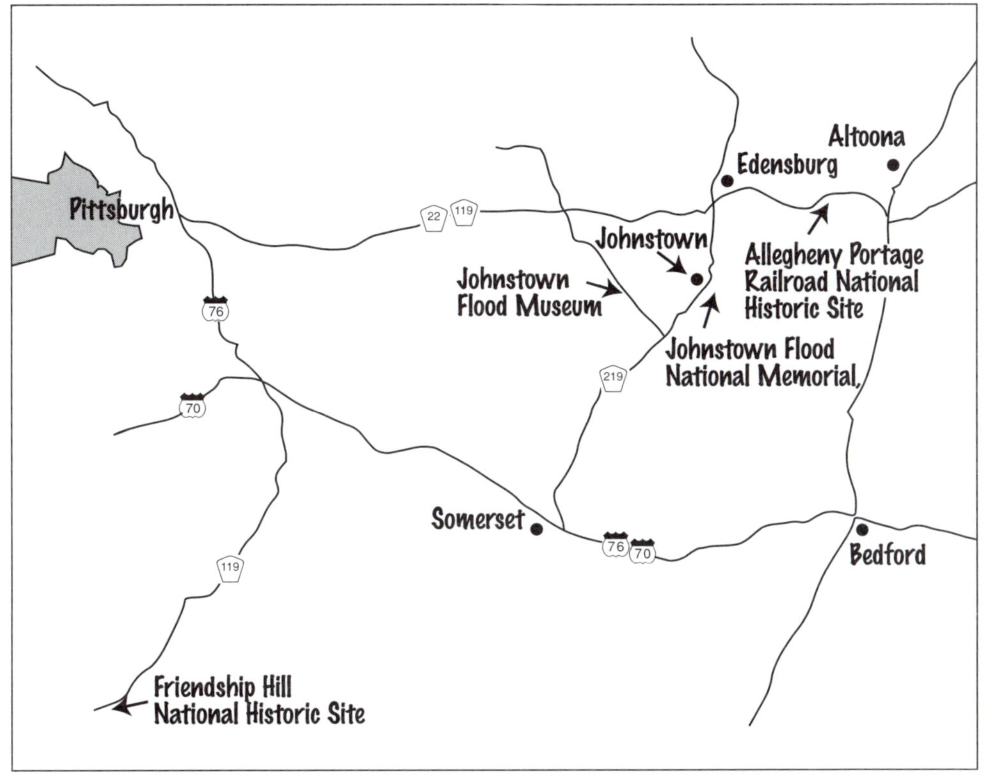

Learn the dramatic story behind the Johnstown Flood. That cataclysmic event can be traced to the building of the Pennsylvania Mainline Canal. Trace the route of the Allegheny Portage Railroad, which carried canal boats over a mountain. The Concorde of its day, the railroad attracted celebrities like Charles Dickens. Visit the home of Albert Gallatin, a financial wizard who first made the case that the federal government should pay for roads and canals.

Mainline Canal

There are few physical remains of Pennsylvania's boldest effort at canal building: the Pennsylvania Mainline Canal, but numbers alone convey a sense of its magnitude. When the Mainline opened in 1835, the route from Philadelphia to Pittsburgh contained 276 miles of canal and 82 miles of railroad track. Coal boats traveled through 174 locks, over 49 aqueducts and through three tunnels, including a 900-foot tunnel four miles east of Johnstown. The project initially cost more than $12 million, and the price tag rose to $16.5 million by 1857.

Fear was the primary motivation for this expensive undertaking. In 1823, two years before the opening of the Erie Canal, a special committee of the Pennsylvania legislature wrote of their state's future, "unless she awakens to a true sense of her situation she will be deprived of sources of public prosperity." Those farsighted leaders had good reasons to be worried that Pennsylvania would lose its economic dominance.

Philadelphia was then the largest city in the country and second only to London in the English-speaking world. But the opening of the Erie Canal soon would threaten that port city's prosperity, by providing an inexpensive way of moving goods to and from the Ohio Valley.

Challenges were also developing to the south. The Baltimore and Ohio Railroad and the Chesapeake and Ohio Canal Company were battling to reach Cumberland, Md., and control the transportation corridor along the Potomac River and west to the Ohio River. The proposed Chesapeake and Delaware Canal, linking the Chesapeake and Delaware Bays, would have its western terminus only a few miles south of Philadelphia.

Washington politicians were responsible for yet another threat. Although the great debate over the federal role in supporting internal improvements wasn't over, Congress had passed legislation stipulating that part of the proceeds of the sale of public lands in the new state of Ohio be used to build roads that would open the eastern seaboard to commerce with new areas of the country. The National Road, the first highway funded under this program, opened in

1818, linking Cumberland, Md., and Wheeling, West Va.,
and offering yet another route west.

The climate was right to promote an outrageously ambitious enterprise: a canal linking Philadelphia to the Ohio River
at Pittsburgh. Canal advocates could easily depict the economic devastation if Philadelphia lost its commercial dominance to the ports of New York City and Baltimore, but no one
could foresee the engineering challenges of the proposed canal.

Open a map of western Pennsylvania to see the most
obvious of those problems: the mountainous terrain between
Hollidaysburg and Johnstown. Canal commissioner Charles
Treziyulney, appointed by the state legislature to recommend
a canal route, refused to accept the easy optimism of the
day, observing, "Here nature has refused to make her usual
kind advances to aid the exertions of man; mountains are
thrown together as if to defy human ingenuity and baffle the
skill of the engineer."

No mountain could discourage Irish immigrant Mathew
Carey, the most energetic of the canal's supporters. An
advocate of economic independence for his adopted country, Carey was a writer, publisher and tireless organizer. With
the Pennsylvania Society for the Promotion of Internal
Improvements, he issued pamphlets, circulated petitions,
wrote newspaper articles and organized mass meetings to
persuade officials to fund a major canal across the state.

The first of a series of acts by the state legislature finally
led to the start of actual construction on July 4, 1826, near
the capitol at Harrisburg. The next year, a second law
authorized two more segments of the Mainline canal and
construction on other canals that greatly expanded the role
of the state in canal-building.

The route, which went along the Susquehanna and
Juaniata Rivers to the Allegheny Mountains and then paral-
leled the Allegheny and Conemaugh Rivers to Pittsburgh,
was filled with engineering difficulties. None was more challenging, however, than the 36 miles from Hollidaysburg to
Johnstown. Construction began before an agreement was
reached about how the mountain would be crossed. A four-
mile tunnel was proposed, with the canal commissioners

*The
Mainline
was the
Concorde of
its day.*

claiming hopefully, "A tunnel is like a well, dug horizontally through a hill or mountain."

A road was also considered, but the final decision was to build a portage railroad. Canal historian Ronald Shaw calls the Allegheny Portage Railroad "one of the great engineering triumphs of the Canal Era." From Hollidaysburg, the train climbed almost 1,400 feet in 10 miles to a point 2,334 feet above sea level, an elevation almost twice that overcome by the Erie Canal in its entire length of 352 miles. The track then descended 1,171 feet in 26 miles to Johnstown.

At Hollidaysburg, the packet boat sections that had traveled from Philadelphia were floated onto railroad cars for the trip over the mountain. Stationary steam engines pulled them from the water, where they were hauled by locomotives to the first incline. In a shed at the foot of the incline, workers hitched three cars at a time to a continuous cable that moved over rollers between the rails. Another stationary steam engine at the top of the incline pulled the cable at a speed of about 4 mph.

The trip to the top of the mountain required five different inclines. Horses or locomotives dragged the cars from one incline to another. The process was reversed on the other side of the mountain. At the Johnstown canal basin, the boat sections were eased into the water, reassembled and floated down the canal to Pittsburgh.

The Mainline was the Concorde of its day. Ulysses S. Grant, Charles Dickens, Jenny Lind, Fanny Kemble and Harriet Beecher Stowe were a few of the luminaries who made the four-day journey, which involved frequent changes from canal boat to rail car and back again.

The trip was exhilarating or arduous, depending on the traveler's temperament. Dickens remembers "the exquisite beauty of the opening day, when light came gleaming off from everything; the lazy motion of the boat...the gliding on at night, so noiselessly, the shining of the bright stars." But another English visitor, Frances Trollope, wrote, "I can hardly imagine any motive of convenience powerful enough to induce me again to imprison myself in a canal boat under ordinary circumstances."

On Board

musing is the look of dismay which each newcomer gives to the confined quarters that present themselves. Those who were so ignorant of the power of compression as to suppose the boat scarce large enough to contain them and theirs, find, with dismay, a respectable colony of old ladies, babies, mothers, big baskets, and carpet bags already established. "Mercy on us!" says one, after surveying the little room, about 10 feet long and six high. "Where are we to sleep tonight?"

Then there is the "turning out scene," when the whole caravan's ejected into the gentlemen's cabin, that the beds may be made... At length, it is announced that all is ready. Forthwith the whole company rush back, and find the walls embellished by a series of little shelves, about a foot wide, each furnished with a mattress and bedding and hooked to the ceiling with a suspiciously slender cord— Direful are the ruminations and exclamations of inexperienced travellers as they eye these very equivocal accommodations. "What sleep up there! The cords will surely break."

— Harriett Beecher Stowe

The canal builders' display of persistence and audacity should have been rewarded with success and riches. However, the Mainline Canal never lived up to its commercial expectations. The portage railroad technology was obsolete within a few years; railroads took away business, and the inclines were slow and expensive to operate. Alvin Harlow writes, "the plain truth was that the Pennsylvania Grand Canal as a freight carrier to the West was not a great success, though it seemed very busy."

In the early 1850s, the state began construction of a new portage railroad without the inclined planes. But even as that work was being completed, the privately owned Pennsylvania Railroad was climbing over the Alleghenies. The canal, which froze over during the winter, couldn't compete with the new mode of transportation that offered faster, year-round service. The portage was abandoned after 23 years of service when the Pennsylvania Railroad bought the Mainline in 1857.

A Born Agitator

At age 79, when Mathew Carey was in the last year of his life, he wrote, "I am in a great manner toothless, a cripple, and half blind. But I find no decay in my intellectual powers."

At a distance of more than 150 years, it's possible to feel the power of this Irish immigrant's indefatigable energy. Before he was 20, his pamphleteering on behalf of Catholics had landed him in trouble with the authorities. Carey fled a threatened prison term for libel, spent time with Benjamin Franklin in Paris and eventually settled in Philadelphia, where he started a bookselling and printing business that became the country's first modern publishing company.

Carey worked tirelessly for Roman Catholic orphans, prison reform, relief of the poor, improved working conditions for women and technical education. But, it was the battle for internal improvements that really captured his heart.

The publisher revived the Chesapeake and Delaware Canal project in 1821, after a series of false starts. He got together a Committee of Five, a group of prominent Philadelphians who agreed that the canal was an economic necessity for their city. They stirred up interest in the project, formed a new canal company board and stood ready to accept the subscriptions they assumed would follow their publicity campaign.

When only $20,000 of the $600,000 needed for construction was raised, Carey threw himself into the fray, organizing a petition drive requesting funds of the Pennsylvania state legislature. Funds were later pledged from the legislatures of Maryland, Pennsylvania and Delaware, contingent on private subscriptions, and Carey again rose to the challenge. He wrote in his diary, "I abandoned everything for this great object—devoted my whole mind to it from an early hour in the morning till late at night—wrote paragraphs from day to day..." His campaign eventually produced subscription pledges of $350,000.

Carey later spearheaded the drive for the Mainline Canal. In 1824, he organized the Pennsylvania Society for the Promotion of Internal Improvements, which lobbied for state support for canals. The society, with Carey's publishing house at its disposal, barraged the public with pamphlets and other materials touting the prosperity that would follow canal construction.

One of the most endearing episodes in Carey's life was his support for John Randel, Jr., a well-regarded engineer hired to build a section of the Chesapeake and Delaware Canal. Randel sued the canal company for breach of contract after being fired by the board. Carey rushed to his defense with a pamphlet, entitled, *Exhibit of the Shocking Oppression and Injustice Suffered by John Randel, Jun....from Judge Wright, Engineer in Chief and the Majority of the Board of Directors."*

Carey tried unsuccessfully to organize a meeting that would enable stockholders to take a position against the decision. An entry in his diary gives a good idea of his contempt for those who turn their eyes from injustice. "It is melancholy to think that such a villainous course of conduct...should be viewed with so much apathy...But what avails feeling, however strong, without effort!"

Carey's own efforts to right a wrong threatened his beloved canal, but his passion for justice overrode any worries that the project might not survive. He was a born agitator—impulsive, persuasive and very appealing.

Allegheny Portage Railroad National Historic Site

Park officials do a good job with their most difficult task: explaining how the 19th-century engineers got the portage railroad up the mountain and down the other side. Get a copy of the free brochure on inclined planes at the visitor's center and then take a look at the working model of a railroad car being pulled up the mountain via inclined planes, while the car's weight is balanced by a descending car. Remains of one of the inclined planes and the old railroad bed are visible on the park grounds.

"The portage railroad was exactly like the space shuttle," says ranger Diane Garcia. "Everyone was thrilled by the new technology at first. In five years, it was old hat and 20 years later, it was obsolete." A 20-minute introductory movie captures the economic importance of the railroad to 19th-century settlers.

Walk a short distance from the visitor's center to the Lemon House, a restored tavern that was a rest and dining stop for railroad passengers. Near a restored bar, a cardboard facsimile of a patron cheerfully toasts a friend. Sheet music is on the piano and newspapers of the day are displayed in the sedate Fancy Parlor, where the women gathered while the men relaxed more boisterously.

The Engine House #6 Exhibit Shelter preserves the remains of the original building at the head of one of the inclined planes. The building contains interactive exhibits on the railroad's technology. Staple Bend Tunnel, the country's first railroad tunnel, is outside the main park area, but rangers lead hikes to the tunnel. They also lead hikes along the 8-mile route from the railroad to Hollidaysburg, the canal town where the journey started over the mountain.

Take a short detour to the nearby Horseshoe Curve National Historic Landmark. The Pennsylvania Railroad made the Mainline Canal obsolete when rails conquered the mountainous terrain between Altoona and Gallitzin. Trains still travel the Horseshoe Curve, which was part of this route.

The park is 12 miles west of Altoona and 10 miles east of Ebensburg on U.S. Route 22. Take the Gallitzin exit. Box 189, Cresson, PA 16630. 814-886-6150. www.nps.gov/alpo

Men of all classes met in taverns along the route of the portage railroad.

Johnstown Flood

More than 2,000 people died in the spring of 1889, in the infamous Johnstown Flood. Efforts to shore up the South Fork dam failed and a body of water with the force of Niagara Falls moved into the thriving steel town. The water had picked up debris for 14 miles before reaching Johnstown. Contemporary accounts describe a rolling 40-foot hill made up of buildings, machinery, freight cars, trees, bridge sections and even animals and people.

The most painful deaths came to those trapped in the debris when it lodged against a railroad bridge. The 45-acre mass was pushed against the bridge by the powerful flood current and bound tight by barbed wire. The oil-soaked jam caught fire and flames spread over the entire expanse of rubble, burning people alive.

The story of the flood is so dramatic that it's easy to overlook an earlier tale: how the dam came to be built. The

Damage from the Johnstown flood.

area west of Johnstown suffered from water shortages during the summer, hardly ideal conditions for a canal. In 1836, just after the opening of the Mainline, the state legislature approved funds to build a reservoir that would provide water for the canal during that dry period.

Work finally began in 1838, but even the dam's early history was ill fated. The project was abandoned for long stretches of time, first because of lack of money and later because of a cholera epidemic. The first state appropriation was for $30,000; the final price tag, nearly $240,000. Fifteen years passed before the dam was finally completed. Six months later, the Pennsylvania Railroad made its first run from Philadelphia to Pittsburgh, sounding the death knell for the Mainline and rendering the dam obsolete for its original purpose.

The Pennsylvania Railroad bought the South Fork Dam as part of a package including the Portage Railroad and the Mainline itself and sold it to a private owner. Eventually the dam ended up as part of the property of the South Fork Fishing and Hunting Club, an exclusive organization with Andrew Carnegie and Andrew Mellon on its membership rolls. A Johnstown businessman, Daniel J. Morrell, warned that the dam might break, but the club president refused requests that it be strengthened.

The horror of the Johnstown Flood captured the imagination of Pulitzer Prize-winning historian David McCullough, whose first book focused on the event, and Charles Guggenheim, whose documentary about the event won an Academy Award. Both film, which is available on video, and book offer dramatic renditions of the tragedy and its aftermath.

Johnstown Flood National Memorial

Operated by the National Park Service, the plain, two-story visitor's center for this attraction is located near the site of the South Fork Dam. On the inside ceiling, the lifesize figure of a young boy appears to be clutching the edge of a roof. The exhibit depicts Victor Heiser's famous ride during the flood. The farm boy survived a long journey through turbulent waters by clinging to the roof of his barn. Visitors can hear a taped account of some of Heiser's memories of the flood.

"Black Friday" is a stunning, 35-minute-long movie that comes with a parental advisory because of its amazing ability to recreate the flood experience. Visitors can also trace the flood's path on a fibre-optic map and join a ranger-led tour of the water's route from the dam.

Exiting U.S. 219 for the Johnstown Memorial, you'll come to the small town of St. Michael. Take a few minutes to visit the property of the South Fork Fishing and Hunting Club, where the Pittsburgh millionaires created an almost inviolable enclave of privilege before the flood. A historical preservation society restored several of the Victorian cottages and has ambitious plans for the clubhouse, which houses a gift shop.

The park is 10 miles northeast of Johnstown. Take U.S. 219 to the Saint Michael/Sideman exit. Head east on PA 869 and turn left onto Lake Road. 733 Lake Road, South Fork 15956. Open year-round. Admission. 814-495-4643. www.nps.gov/jofl/

Dramatic ceiling exhibit of Victor Heiser's wild ride during the flood. He appears in the upper right corner.

Johnstown Flood Museum

This museum, operated by the Johnstown Area Heritage Association, screens the Oscar-winning documentary of the flood and offers a multi-media show that allows visitors to experience the flood in 3-D. Exhibits tell the story of the town's later reconstruction.

For another perspective on Johnstown history, walk a few blocks to the entrance of the Johnstown Inclined Plane, billed by the Guinness Book of Records as the steepest vehicular inclined plane in the world. Ride almost 900 feet to a visitor's center, where windows frame Johnstown and exhibits tell its story. The inclined railroad was built in 1891 after the flood, when residents went in search of higher ground on which to build their new homes.

304 Washington St., Johnstown 15901. Admission. 888-222-1889. www.ctcnet.net/jaha/pages/jfm.

Friendship Hill National Historic Site

Swiss-born Albert Gallatin gave up wealth and social position to move to the United States because of "a love of independence in the freest country of the universe."

Gallatin's affection for his new country took the form of the unglamourous effort to reduce the country's debt and establish accountability for disbursements. President Jefferson appointed him Secretary of the Treasury in 1801 and by the time Gallatin left office eight years later, he had reduced the public debt by $14 million and built up a surplus. Later, the versatile immigrant played a key role in negotiating the Treaty of Ghent, which ended the War of 1812.

A government report, however, represents Gallatin's contribution to canal history. The origin of the document goes back to President Jefferson's comments in his sixth annual message that public revenues should be used for "roads, rivers, canals and other such objects of public improvement." States quickly sent requests for such support to Congress. John Quincy Adams spoke against their funding and instead introduced legislation asking that Gallatin, as

Secretary of the Treasury, develop a plan describing transportation projects worthy of federal funds.

The Report of the Secretary of the Treasury on the Subject of Roads and Canals, sent to Congress in 1808, became a famous document in the subsequent debate about federal support for internal improvements. Gallatin proposed a comprehensive building program with a price tag of $20 million and a 10-year period of activity. He recommended four canals along the eastern coast: the Cape Cod canal; the Delaware and Raritan Canal in New Jersey; the Chesapeake and Delaware Canal, and the Dismal Swamp Canal, connecting Chesapeake Bay to Albermarle Sound.

The historic site, operated by the National Park Service, preserves Gallatin's country estate . Throughout the year, a self-guided audio house tour is offered, along with changing exhibits. During the summer season, staff provide lectures, special programs and concerts. The park has 10 miles of nature trails.

Three miles north of Point Marion on SR 166 or 12 miles south of Uniontown. One Washington Parkway, Farmington 15437, 724-725-9190. www.nps.gov/frhi

Other small canal parks and museums are scattered around the state. New York has several sites commemorating Pennsylvania's canal history. The locations described below begin in eastern Pennsylvania and move westward.

Schuylkill Canal and Navigation

This waterway, which stretches 108 miles from Port Carbon to Philadelphia, was a combination of 46 miles of slack water navigation, for which dams and locks were constructed on the Schuylkill River, and 62 miles of canal travel.

Its earliest history was linked with the Union Canal. Pennsylvania chartered two companies in 1792 to build a navigable waterway between the Schuylkill and Susquehanna Rivers, improve the Schuylkill from Norristown to Reading and build a canal from the Delaware River to Norristown. The ill-fated effort ran out of money. In 1815, Pennsylvania chartered the Schuylkill Navigation Company to complete the work on the river. The waterway, which operated until 1931, was used primarily to bring anthracite from the coal regions to Philadelphia.

In 1982, when Pennsylvania invited Upper Providence Township to lease the state-owned area, the windows of the gutted lockhouse were boarded up and marked with bullet holes. Within two years, local officials and volunteers had repaired and rented the lockhouse and removed tons of trash. A year later, the volunteer advisory committee incorporated as the non-profit Schuylkill Canal Association and later won the Phoenixville Chamber of Commerce Civil Betterment Award.

The recreational area offers 2.5 miles of canal and towpath, a historic lock, a 1836 lockhouse, picnic groves, canoe access to the canal and links to other hiking trails.

Take 422 west from King of Prussia to route 29. Exit at the Collegeville exit and travel south on 29 to Mont Clare.

C. Howard Hiester Canal Center

The namesake for this museum had a life-long fascination with canals. When the Schuylkill Navigation Company closed its headquarters in 1927, Hiester retrieved tools, photos, ledgers and correspondence, which had been thrown into the canal bed for fill. Those items became the core of a collection that eventually totaled more than 1,000 items and included anchors, tools of all descriptions, tickets, stamps and a houseboat. The Berks County Park and Recreation Department agreed to operate the canal center as part of the Berks County Heritage Center.

Berks County Heritage Center, R.D. #5, Box 272, Sinking Spring 19608 Admission. Open May-October. 610-374-8839.

Union Canal

The Union Canal had a glorious beginning, but a troubled life. William Penn was the first to propose a waterway linking the Schuylkill and Susquehanna Rivers. Astronomer David Rittenhouse and William Smith, provost of the University of Pennsylvania, conducted the first canal survey, when they followed Penn's proposed route from Reading on the Schuylkill River to Middletown on the Susquehanna.

The earliest construction effort began in 1792 and ended two years later, when the canal companies ran out of money, after completing only 15 miles of work. Twenty-seven years passed before the next attempt, which faltered because of inadequate financing. Fears caused by the imminent completion of the Erie Canal loosened the state's purse strings, and an influx of public money enabled the Union Canal Company to continue its work.

In 1828, three years after the Erie Canal opened, the first boat traveled from Philadelphia to Middletown, using the 81-mile long canal. The journey took five days, during which the boat passed through 94 locks and climbed more than 300 feet to the canal's summit at Lebanon. The initial price tag for the canal was $6 million, but that figure eventually doubled.

The channel and locks of the Union Canal were too narrow for the boats that used the Schuylkill Navigation system and the Mainline. The canal company spent an additional $6 million to widen the channel, but the enlargement was not completed until 1856.

Frequent flooding exacerbated the canal's problems. The 22-mile long Pine Grove feeder canal brought water westward from a large reservoir to the summit of the Union Canal. A flood destroyed the feeder in 1863. The Union Canal never recovered economically and was abandoned in 1885.

Union Canal Park, which is maintained by the Lebanon County Historical Society, is the site of the oldest existing canal tunnel in the United States. Crew poled canal boats through the 606-foot canal tunnel, while the mules were walked over the mountain. During the Depression, restoration was done by workers under the aegis of the Works Progress Administration. Water flows through the length of the tunnel and seasonal boat trips are offered on request.

The park is at the corner of 25th St. and Union Canal Drive, about one mile northwest of Lebanon.

Erie Extension Canal

A small canal museum tells the story of the Erie Extension Canal, which consisted of a series of connected slackwater and canal projects designed to link the town of Erie with the Mainline Canal. The first of these projects, authorized in 1826, connected Conneaut Lake, Meadville and Franklin by a feeder canal along French Creek. Five years later, navigational improvements began along the Beaver and Chaining Rivers to Pulaski. An extension from Pulaski to Conneaut Lake was approved in 1836 and two years later contracts were let for a 45-mile segment to make the final connection between Conneaut Lake and Erie.

By 1843, the state had spent more than $4 million on construction and the canal was still unfinished. The entire project was turned over to a private company, which invested another $.5 million in the project, and finally opened the 136-mile canal and slackwater navigation in 1844.

Delaware Aqueduct

The Delaware Aqueduct spans the Upper Delaware National
Scenic and Recreational River, connecting Lackawaxen and
Minisink Ford, New York. The structure, which also goes by
the name of Roebling Bridge, is the oldest suspension bridge
in the United States. It has four spans of 188 feet, each sus-
pended on 8.5-inch wire cables. The wooden portions of the
bridge have been replaced, but the cables are visible.

John Roebling designed the aqueduct in 1846 to solve a
problem for the Delaware and Hudson Canal Company.
Although the canal had been operating successfully for 18
years, a section where the boats crossed the Delaware River
was a persistent trouble spot. Timber rafts rushing down the
river collided with slow canal boats, which relied on a rope
ferry to get across the river. The rope ferry was useless when
the water was high. Roebling decided to build the canal
above the water, permitting ice flows and timber rafts to
pass beneath.

*From Port Jervis, NY take route 97 northwest to the bridge.
The Tollhouse Visitor Contact Center can be reached at
717-685-4871.*

The Delaware Aqueduct is the oldest suspension bridge in the United States

Delaware and Hudson Canal

The 108-mile canal was built to move coal from the
Pennsylvania's Lackawaxen Valley to New York City.
Starting in Honesdale, the canal followed the Delaware
River to Port Jervis, where it turned northeast up the
Neversink and Rondout valleys to Kingston, New York on
the Hudson River. A 16-mile gravity railroad with coal cars
climbed 850 feet over the mountains from Carbondale to
Honesdale, where the coal was loaded on canal boats. The
canal was constructed between 1825 and 1829.

The Delaware and Hudson Canal Society operates the museum in the small town of High Falls, where a series of five locks compensated for an elevation drop of 70 feet. Visitors can trace the canal on a wall map from Honesdale along a course parallel to four bodies of water: the Lackawaxen, Delaware and Neversink Rivers and the Rondout Creek to its terminus at Kingston at sea level.

A diorama shows how a gravity railroad moved coal from the mines in Carbondale to the canal at Honesdale. Other dioramas show living quarters on the canal boats, boat building and canal traffic. With a brochure and map, visitors can tour the five locks located in High Falls, the towpath past the Locktender's Cottage and stone abutments that supported a wooden aqueduct. The 1797 DePuy Canal House, once a canal tavern and a now a four-star restaurant, is located next to lock 16.

From Kingston at New York State Thruway exit 19, take route 28 several hundred feet to the exit for route 209 south. Drive about 10 miles and turn left on route 213 into High Falls. Hours vary. Mohonk Road, High Falls, NY 12440. 914-687-9311.

D&H Canal Park-Neversink Valley Area Museum

This 300-acre county-owned park includes a one- mile section of the canal with the remains of a canal aqueduct and lock, a lockkeeper's house, canal store, blacksmith's house and full-size canal barge replica. The museum offers a large wall-size map of the canal, videos, artifacts, a working lock model, photographs and information on canal technology and history. An activity center for children includes a working rudder, tiller, bilge pump, pulley and other learning devices.

From Port Jervis, NY take route 209 10 miles north to Hoag Rd. Cuddebackville, NY 12729. Admission. Seasonal hours for museum. 914-754-8870.

Events

Elderhostel

For those 50 years of age and over, this educational program
offers a one-week course at Lafayette College in Easton on
towpath canals and a one-week course at Jim Thorpe on the
town's history. Call 617-426-8056 for a catalog.

Canal History and Technology Symposium

Sponsored by the Center for Canal History and Technology
and Lafayette College, this annual event was first held in
1982. The meeting, which is held at the National Canal
Museum, attracts 100 to 200 canal scholars and historians,
whose papers are published in a volume of proceedings. Call
610-515-8000.

Canal Festival

This annual event celebrated its 20th anniversary on June
28, 1998. Held in Hugh Moore Park in Easton, it offers
jazz, folk music, arts and crafts, open hearth cooking and
living history encampments. Canal workers reminisce about
the old days and canal advocates bring the public up to date
on restoration efforts. Call 610-515-8000.

Lehigh River Sojourn

Each June, the Wildlands Conservancy sponsors a 6-day trip
to highlight the joys of river activities. Participants can join in
segments of the event or make the entire journey. Activities
include nature hikes, whitewater rafting from White Haven
to Drake's Creek, a bike ride from Rockport to Jim Thorpe, a
canoe trip from Jim Thorpe to Walnutport and canoeing on
the Lehigh Canal. The Walnutport Canal Association hosts
the group at the lockhouse. Call 610-965-4397.

Schuylkill Canal Day

On the last Sunday in June, the Schuylkill Canal
Association hosts a celebration on the banks of the
Schuylkill in St. Michael's Park, near Mont Clare. Activities
include art exhibits, canoe races, fire company hose competition and food. Call 610-933-8036.

Walk the Delaware Canal

Each fall, the Friends of the Delaware Canal sponsors a five-part walk of the 60-mile canal towpath. On successive Saturdays, the group meets at specified locations, walks from 11 to 14 miles and then carpools to the starting point. Those who go the distance are awarded a Lehigh Coal and Navigation Company stock certificate. Call 215-862-2021.

Walnutport Canal Festival

On the third Sunday in October, the Walnutport Canal Association hosts a festival with arts and crafts, historical exhibits, food and activities for children. Call 610-767-5817.

Organizations

Delaware and Hudson Canal Historical Society
P.O. Box 23
High Falls, NY 12440
914-687-9311

Delaware and Lehigh Canal National Heritage Corridor
Commission
10 East Church St., P-206
Bethlehem, PA 18018
610-861-9345

Friends of Delaware Canal
145 South Main St.
New Hope, PA 18938
215-862-2021

Lehigh Canal Park Recreation Commission
1311 Main Road
Lehighton, PA 18235

Old Freemansburg Association
219 Main St.
Freemansburg, PA 18071

Pennsylvania Canal Society
P.O. Box 2537
West Chester, PA 19380-2537

Schuylkill Canal Association, Inc.
P.O. Box 3
Mont Clare, PA 19453

Walnutport Canal Association
417 Lincoln Ave.
Walnutport, PA 18088
610-767-5817

Wildlands Conservancy
3701 Orchid Place
Emmaus, PA 18049
610-965-4397

Tourist Information

Pennsylvania Tourism
800-847-4872
www.state.pa.us/visit

Bucks County Tourist Commission, Inc.
P.O. Box 912, Dept. 73
Doylestown, PA 18901
800-836-2825

Bureau of State Parks
P.O. Box 855
Harrisburg, PA 17105
888-PA-PARKS

Bureau of Travel Marketing
453 Forum Building
Harrisburg, PA 17120
800-237-4363

Carbon County Tourist Promotion Agency
CRRNJ Railway Station
P.O. Box 90
Jim Thorpe, PA 18229
717-325-3673

Lehigh Valley Convention and Visitor's Bureau
P.O. Box 20785
Lehigh Valley, PA 18002
800-747-0561
http://lehighvalleypa.org

Publications

Barber, David G. *A Guide to the Lehigh Canal: Lower and Upper Divisions*. North Wales, Pa.: Delaware Valley Chapter of Appalachian Mountain Club, 1992.

This mile-by-mile description of the canal route has accounts of the Switchback Railroad and Josiah White's career. Includes maps and photographs.

Cochran, Thomas. *Pennsylvania*. New York: W.W. Norton. 1978.

D&L Trail Workbook. Rivers, Trails and Conservation Assistance Program, National Park Service, 1996.

Metz, Lance. *Cap't Sherman's Guide to Hugh Moore Park*. Easton, Pa.: Center for Canal History and Technology, 1988.

This 60-page booklet provides more information than the title suggests. It covers the history of area canals and has a bibliography and very useful glossary.

Morton, Eleanor. *Josiah White: Prince of Pioneers*. New York: Stephen Daye Press, 1946.

You can guess the approach of this book by the subtitle. It offers a fascinating, but idealized, portrait of White, which includes excerpts from his journals.

Rivinus, Willis M. *Guide to the Delaware Canal.* Self-published, 1964

This mile-by-mile account of the canal towpath has been revised six times, most recently in 1993. It's the basic text for towpath walkers.

Rivinus, Willis M. (Ed.) *The Complete Guide to the Delaware and Lehigh National Heritage Corridor.* Bethlehem, Pa.: Lehigh River Foundation, 1994.

This guide is a collection of pieces in four categories: Delaware and Lehigh Heritage Corridor; Unique Trips and Tours; Historic Heritage, and Attractions, Activities and Events. Much of the material is useful, although the quality of the articles is uneven. The bibliography offers good information about books on specific canals.

Shank, William H. *The Amazing Pennsylvania Canals.* York, Pa., American Canal and Transportation Center, 1960.

This is the basic text for virtually every writer about Pennsylvania canals. Its comprehensive map showing Pennsylvania canals and canal-related railroads frequently appears in other books. Reprinted in 1991.

The 184-mile Chesapeake and Ohio Canal begins in the heart of the nation's capital and passes by small-town America, rural countryside and stunning river vistas.

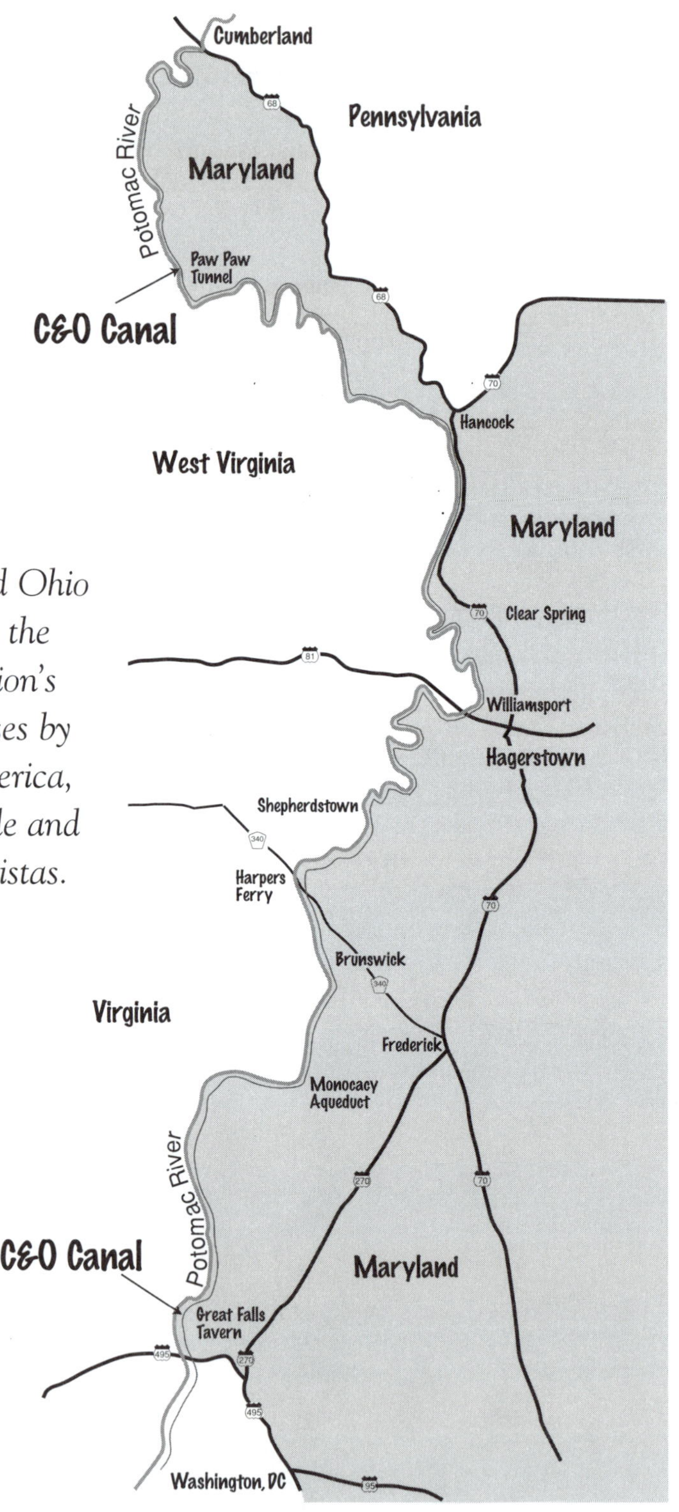

Maryland

Canal history in Maryland has always been shaped by the state's proximity to the nation's capital. Before George Washington was president of the country, he was president of the Patowmack Company, a predecessor to the Chesapeake and Ohio Canal Company. The canal itself was built with $1 million in federal funds, even though other canals of the same period were dependent on private investment or state funding.

William O. Douglas relaxed from his deliberations as a Supreme Court Justice by hiking along the undeveloped canal towpath. When the National Park Service announced plans to build a parkway that would threaten this place of solace, he rallied environmentalists who joined him on a well-publicized 184-mile walk from one end of the canal to the other. In 1971, Congress designated the area around the canal the Chesapeake and Ohio Canal National Historical Park.

By contrast, very little of the 14-mile Chesapeake and Delaware Canal runs through Maryland. The canal's western terminus is at Chesapeake City, a sleepy shore town that lies about 200 miles northeast of Washington, D.C. The area is accessible only by automobile and attracts a tiny number of visitors in comparison with the renowned C&O Canal. But, the C&D also was influenced by what happened in the capital. In fact, it was debate about funding for this canal that precipitated the famous "Report on Roads and Canals," in 1808, in which the Secretary of the Treasury Albert Gallatin argued that internal improvements merit federal support.

During the Civil War, troops and supplies flowed through the canal to the Army of the Potomac, which was defending the capitol. During World War I and again in World War II, munitions were transported through the canal to avoid a hazardous trip on the Atlantic Ocean.

Maryland canal attractions are wonderfully eclectic. Visitors flock to the well-known attractions at the lower end of the C&O canal park. Canal boats leave from both Georgetown in Washington and the Great Falls area in Maryland. On a single weekend, park rangers might offer six or seven events. Boats are available for rent at Fletcher's and Swain's boathouses.

Between three and four million visits are paid to the park each year, but more than three-quarters of them are to a 15-mile stretch that begins in Georgetown. Despite the park's popularity, it's possible to enjoy many of its attractions in virtual solitude. Go upstream a few miles to White's Ferry, or travel further to the beautiful Monocacy Aqueduct and the Paw Paw Tunnel, an engineering marvel that nearly bankrupted the canal company. At the canal's terminus in western Maryland, the small city of Cumberland shows the traces of historic events going back to the French and Indian War.

The Chesapeake and Delaware Canal offers an entirely different set of experiences. Visitors can watch large ocean vessels as they float down the busiest canal in the country. The C&D is more profitable today than it was during the canal era and is constantly being enlarged, refurbished and improved.

Despite the canal's commercial success, however, most area attractions have a small-town flavor. Museums that tell the stories of the C&D and the Susquehanna and Tidewater Canal are modest, but effective. Havre de Grace and Chesapeake City boast waterfront views, historic architecture and a good mix of establishments devoted to tourists and to their own residents.

Chesapeake and Ohio Canal

George Washington was rewarded for his service in the French and Indian War with large land grants in the Ohio Valley. The shrewd businessman bought even more land from his fellow veterans who had received similar, but smaller, benefits. The origin of the Chesapeake and Ohio Canal can be traced back to Washington's desire to exploit the commercial possibilities of his western holdings by linking the Potomac River to the tributaries of the Ohio River.

Washington began his efforts to open a waterway to the west even before the Revolutionary War, when he introduced a bill into Virginia's House of Burgess to promote the improvement and navigation of the Potomac River for 150 miles above tidewater. After the war, he became the first president of the Patowmack Company, which was established for the same purposes as his earlier failed legislation. Company directors planned to build skirting canals around the river channel at its most treacherous rapids: Little Falls, Great Falls, Seneca Falls and two areas near Harpers Ferry, West Va.

At the time the company was founded, engineers were just beginning to understand the difficulties of creating navigable waterways. The company's situation became even more precarious when Washington moved on to an even greater challenge: the U.S. presidency. He kept up with canal activities during his two terms in office, but work proceeded slowly.

When Washington died in 1799, the company was out of money. The Virginia and Maryland legislatures eventually appropriated sufficient funds to complete the work at Great Falls, where the river drops 75 feet in the space of a mile. By 1808, there were five short canals between Washington and a point above Harpers Ferry, West Va.

Frequent flooding interfered with boat traffic and Virginia congressman Charles Mercer soon realized that if a better route were not developed, the Mid-Atlantic area would lose its opportunities to develop western trade. He convened a convention in 1823 of other regional leaders

who were also worried about the challenges of New York's
Erie and Pennsylvania's Mainline canals. They came up with
a competing route that would run 341 miles from
Georgetown along the Potomac River to Cumberland, Md.,
where it would travel west and connect with the headwaters
of the Monongahela River.

Even from those early days, the fate of the canal was
linked to the federal government and presidential politics.
United States engineers surveyed the proposed route and
came up with an estimate of $22 million. President John
Quincy Adams, who had pledged federal support for internal improvements, hadn't bargained for that kind of expen-
diture and quickly told the engineers to reconsider. Their
new estimate for the total route was about half the first figure. The cost of the first section, from Georgetown to
Cumberland, was estimated at $4.5 million.

President Adams claimed it was the greatest moment of
his life, when he dug into the ground to begin work on the
project on July 4, 1828 and he had some reason to be hope-
ful. Congress had come up with an unprecedented $1 mil-
lion in support. Maryland subscribed $.5 million and the
cities of Washington, Georgetown and Alexandria together
committed $1.5 million.

On that same July day, however, Charles Carroll broke
ground for the Baltimore and Ohio Railroad in Baltimore.
The two companies battled for the next 15 years to become
the primary trade route to the west. The most expensive of
these altercations took place over the right of way at the
small town of Point of Rocks, which has only a narrow passage between the river and a mountainous ridge. After a four-
year legal struggle, the courts ruled for the canal company.

Costs far exceeded the original projections. In March
1835, the Maryland legislature approved a loan of $2 million
to complete work to Cumberland; by 1836 the infusion of
funds had run out and work was again delayed. When the
B&O Railroad reached Cumberland in 1842, 18 miles of the
canal in Allegany County were incomplete and the canal
company was in debt. Private investors and the state legislature saved the project, although the canal was never completed beyond Cumberland.

The canal was profitable only during the 1870s. During its peak year, 1875, more than 500 boats carried nearly a million tons of goods such as coal, flour, wheat, lumber and corn. The canal company began a financial decline in 1877 and eventually went into receivership to its rival, the Baltimore and Ohio Railroad. The federal government bought the canal from the railroad for $2 million in 1938.

An Unsung Hero

Without the leadership of Charles F. Mercer, it's doubtful there would have been a Chesapeake & Ohio Canal. The dour legislator schemed, maneuvered, cajoled and lobbied to get the necessary funds and approvals for construction and then headed the Chesapeake and Ohio Canal Company, as its workers raced the Baltimore and Ohio Railroad to Cumberland.

But today, Mercer receives none of the acclaim of the Erie Canal's De Witt Clinton or Pennsylvania's Josiah White. Even his contemporaries couldn't bring themselves to grant the man his due. After five years as canal company president, Mercer was forced out of the position in 1833, sacrificed to the political need to appease the new Andrew Jackson administration.

He was a melancholy man, nicknamed Dick Doleful by a cousin. Mercer poignantly spoke of his own "solitary and friendless" character and inability to experience happiness. Although a member of the Virginia House of Delegates and later, the U.S. House of Representatives, he had none of the legend-inspiring flamboyance of politicians like Henry Clay or Davy Crockett. He gave his only book the bleak title, *An Exposition of the Weakness and Inefficiency of the Government of the United States of America.*

The legislator was a man of his times, who held views that grate on modern sensibilities. A staunch Federalist, Mercer was against eliminating the property requirement for the vote, saying of the so-called common men, "Ignorant from birth and habit, they cannot judge of the wise and proper plans for improving the country."

A natural opponent of Thomas Jefferson, he berated the

Republicans for telling the working class "that they are not only as good as the independent and high classes, but better, because they work and produce what others consume and profit by to grow rich upon..." Sort through the syntax and you'll find that Mercer is griping because the Republicans praised workers for creating the profits enjoyed by the upper class.

Mercer was also fixated on a cause that seems particularly odious today: colonization. He led a movement to pay free blacks to emigrate to a settlement in Africa, a goal that was more important to him than the canal. Mercer said, "There is no internal improvement, not the union of all the waters of the Globe [that] is half so important to Virginia as the removal of the colored race from her bosom."

Look beyond these statements, however, and you'll find a complicated man who wrestled honestly with the issues of his day. Mercer accurately predicated that a new type of poverty would accompany industrialization and worried about its consequences. Although verbally cringing at the behavior of the working class, he spoke in behalf of their education, proclaiming that "It is education, national education alone that can prevent crimes."

Mercer formed an unstable alliance with his enemy Jefferson to persuade the Virginia Legislature to provide financial support for public education. The two men split over which branch should receive the bulk of the funds. The patrician Mercer advocated for primary schools, while Jefferson undertook what now seems to be an elitist defense of support for universities.

Even Mercer's views about colonization seem more subtle on a closer look. A slave owner himself, he called slavery the "foulest of all deformities" and like many other slaveholders claimed to want it abolished. He thought that free blacks should be paid to return to Africa because their skin color would keep them part of a permanent under class in the United States.

Although the legislator had ample opportunities to profit personally from his close ties to financiers, Mercer remained free of charges of corruption and for much of his life struggled with debt. His energetic efforts in support of internal improvements were rooted in a view that the development of American industry was the only way to make the United States a strong independent nation. Who now can say he was wrong?

Chesapeake and Ohio Canal National Historical Park

This is my park and it's possible that a million or so other people feel the same way about it. Its popularity was evident immediately after the Blizzard of '96 produced floods that wrecked the towpath, damaged historic structures and left mountains of trash and debris. Within a matter of days, more than 6,000 people called, wrote and signed up on the Internet to help with restoration.

The park might never have come into existence without the advocacy of Supreme Court Justice William Douglas. In 1954, when editors of the *Washington Post* wrote in favor of a National Park Service plan to build a parkway along the towpath, Douglas challenged them to walk the full length of towpath and discover "a place not yet marred by the roar of wheels and sound of horns." Thirty-seven newspaper reporters, conservationists and a few kibitzers set out from Cumberland on March 21 and nine eventually completed the entire walk to Georgetown. Douglas ended the journey perched on the stern of the *Canal Clipper*, waving his hat in response to a cheering crowd, as the boat was pulled by mules along the canal.

By the end of the trip, the *Post's* editors favored a compromise between the two views concerning the parkway and they had learned some valuable trail lessons. They concluded, "Out here, the first signs of spring seem far more important than the antics of self-inflated wild men or what Congress does with the tax bill."

Despite the walk's dramatic conclusion, nearly 20 years passed before Congress acted to designate the Chesapeake & Ohio Canal National Historical Park. The park owes its existence to supporters who generated publicity with annual treks on the towpath and to politicians like Gilbert Gude who maneuvered, persuaded and cajoled to get legislation passed.

The park stretches 184.5 miles from Georgetown in downtown Washington, D.C., to Cumberland in western Maryland. Well-maintained hiker-biker campsites at con-

venient locations have helped to produce thousands of
Washingtonians devoted to annual park rituals. They bike
the full distance; set aside weekends to walk different sections of the towpath or line up to ride a canal boat.

The Great Falls Tavern Visitors Center offers a good
introduction to the park. Park rangers offer an imaginative
array of opportunities to learn about the history—both natural and human—of the area. Costumed interpreters
accompany passengers on the mule-drawn *Canal Clipper*
that operates along the canal in season. The area is one of
the few places where canoeing is possible on the canal,
although the nearby Potomac River is a popular canoeing
spot for much of the canal's length.

It only takes a couple of hours from the Washington
area to travel by car to the canal's end. But 80 percent of

the park's visits are to a small section close to the metropoli-
tan area: a 15-mile segment of the towpath that extends
from Georgetown to the Great Falls Tavern Visitors Center.
On weekends, area residents think locally and end up vying
for parking spots at the lower end of the park, leaving
uncrowded sections of the towpath at the upper end. Hike,
bike, ride on horseback or even ski down the towpath. Here
are a few of the attractions as you travel west from Great
Falls Tavern Visitors Center.

*Great Falls Tavern Visitors Center is at 11710 MacArthur Blvd,
Potomac. 301-299-3613. For information about the Canal
Clipper call 301-299-2026. Admission*

In the spring of 1998, one of the canal's contemporary success stories took place at an out-of-the way site about 40
miles northwest of Washington. The First Lady arrived to
announce that the **Monocacy Aqueduct** had been named
by the National Trust for Historic Preservation to its annual
list of America's 11 Most Endangered Historic Places.

The aqueduct is a 516-foot bridge that was built to
carry the canal (including boats and mules) over the

*The National Trust
for Historic
Preservation named
the Monocacy
Aqueduct to its list
of most endangered
historic structures in
1998.*

Monocacy River. Irish and Welsh laborers had hauled quartz from nearby Sugar Loaf Mountain to construct the aqueduct's seven 54-foot arches. The imposing structure took five years to complete and was called one of Maryland's seven wonders and depicted on silver platters used in state banquets. Confederate troops tried to dynamite the aqueduct to stop the movement of Union soldiers, but were stymied by the workmanship and dense stone.

But the canal's frequent floods began to bring about what the troops were unable to accomplish. By 1972, when Hurricane Agnes hit the area, the aqueduct had already been repeatedly battered by floating logs and debris during earlier floods.   National Park Service staff were afraid the structure might collapse and encased it in an ugly harness. They estimated that repair could cost as much as $28 million, but showed no urgency about getting the expensive work started. When funds for the aqueduct were budgeted, the money was reallocated to park areas with noisier constituencies.

In 1995, Carl Linden formed the Uphold the Monocacy Campaign as a project of the C&O Canal Association. The group enlisted the help of a popular former congressman, Gilbert Gude, who had sponsored the legislation creating the canal park in 1971. Almost immediately after the committee got to work, back-to-back snow blizzards destroyed many sections of the park. Congress appropriated $22 million to repair damage, but the aqueduct was once again shortchanged. Undaunted the group pressed on, securing support from the American Society of Civil Engineers and persuading park officials to undertake a study that would provide a new cost estimate.

National Trust President Richard Moe picked up a brochure about the fundraising campaign from a local library, asked for a tour and was sold on the project. Since Clinton's arrival, park officials have come up with a more palatable figure for stabilization — $5.6 million as opposed to the earlier figure of $28 million — but the association continues to struggle to make the aqueduct a priority. Linden says, "Aqueduct stabilization is in the park budget for 2004, but we're pushing for 2001."

Association members also continue to dream big dreams. If they can get Hillary Clinton to the aqueduct, they reason, why not the environmental artist Christo? They plan to ask him to wrap the aqueduct as he did the famed Pont Neuf, a bridge in Paris.

To reach the Monocacy Aqueduct from the Beltway near Washington, D.C., take 270 to 28. Continue on 28 through Poolesville, passing through Dickerson. Go under the railroad overpass about 100 yards, make a left onto Mouth of Monocacy Road and travel 1.5 miles.

Brunswick became a bustling center as a railroad town after the Baltimore and Ohio Railroad gained ascendency over the canal. Residents haven't forgotten that glorious time. The restaurant on the town's outskirts is called Tracks End; the local liquor store is Iron Horse Spirits, and the town diner, the Silver Rail. Fans cheer for the Railroaders at high school football games and turn out for the annual Railroad Days festival each fall.

The main attraction for outsiders, in addition to the canal itself, is the **Brunswick Railroad Museum** , which contains displays of clothing, housewares, medicine and an exhibit about the canal. Begin with the slide show on the first floor, which describes how Brunswick's fortunes were affected by events beyond the control of its residents and the town became a place for people who work elsewhere.

Local historian Eleanor Milligan became intrigued with the "little snippets of stories" she heard from the wives of Brunswick railroad men. The details of life in a railroad town literally were gritty: women used to time their washing around train schedules because the arrival of a train would release clouds of soot. Milligan conducted a series of inter-views with these women and used excerpts from them to introduce museum exhibits. The text for one exhibit begins, "I took a job to keep me busy. I had my own paycheck and he had his. He wasn't home much."

On the top floor of the museum is a model railroad that has been a work in progress for more than 20 years. The waist-high track nearly fills the room and would stretch for one-third of a mile if extended. The accompanying hand-

The railroad even has a Howard Johnson's restaurant.

out defiantly proclaims, "The model railroad is not finished."

However, it's hard to imagine what more can be added. Houses, cars, trucks, fire stations, cows, trees, bridge, stores, schools and restaurants line the tracks. With the push of a button, the display comes to life: a cow moos, a carousel turns, whistles blow, the high school band plays and a light flashes, simulating fire in a burning home. One button even produces the familiar sound of a frustrated driver trying to get his car started.

From Frederick, take 340 west to 17 east. Museum is at 40 West Potomac St., Brunswick 21716. Hours vary. 301-834-7100.

Even the local McDonald's honors **Williamsport's** canal heritage with a wall mural of a canal boat called Big Mac. Within walking distance of the compact downtown area is one of the most beautiful stretches of the canal park. The Conococheague Aqueduct provides a graceful entrance into the area, and the Cushwa Basin has just been rewatered. Park officials stubbornly persist with restoration efforts, despite periodic flooding.

The **Williamsport Town Museum** is located off East Potomac Street in what was formerly the dairy barn of historic

Springfield Farm. George Washington was courted at the farm by the local elite who hoped Williamsport would become the country's capital. One very large room contains exhibits of local history, including canal memorabilia. Check at the park's visitor's center for hours for the museum.

The National Park Service operates a one-room museum in the Cushwa Warehouse, near the Conococheague Aqueduct. Two videos offer different perspectives on the canal. After a long search, NPS staff unearthed the only film footage that shows the canal in operation. Made by the Thomas Edison Film Company in 1917, the 8-minute film shows a canal boat pulled by mules, a pipe-smoking canoeist complete with handlebar mustache and scenes of a turn-of-the-century Harpers Ferry. TV personality Charles Kuralt narrates the second video, a modern valentine to the canal.

Hancock's chief attraction is a series of inexpensive restaurants. They line Main Street and include Weavers, featuring pan fried chicken, country ham and home-baked pastries, and Park-n-Dine, which claims to serve 1,000 pounds of turkey, ham and beef each week. The owners either have never heard of cholesterol or are ignoring the bad news. Weekly specials include old favorites like ham and cabbage, ham pot pie, swiss steak and pot roast. Visit one of these restaurants and you'll be honoring a long tradition. The National Pike, the country's first federally funded highway, is the predecessor of Hancock's Main Street. Travelers such as George Washington, Andrew Jackson and Henry Clay stopped in the town for a meal.

The **Town Museum** offers a good chance to explore Hancock's history. Located at the corner of High St. and Pennsylvania Ave., it fills one large room in the basement of the municipal building. A well-designed display of antique tools is on one wall, featuring a canal horn that was used to call the lockkeeper when a boat captain wanted passage. The eclectic collection includes a wooden meat grinder, baby carriage, antique clothing, Hancock matchbooks, canal art and other items. A transportation collection, documenting the importance of the railroad, is being developed in an adjoining room. Open April through October. 1st and 3rd Sundays. 2-4 p.m.

Bill's Place, which is by the canal near Hancock, is one of those word-of-mouth establishments that now has been discovered by the *Washington Post*. The ceiling of this restaurant/bar/store is covered with dollar bills (reportedly 6,000 of them) left by customers who wanted to have a dollar to buy a beer in case they were broke on their next visit. The food is simple and cheap; your companions will be local hunters, fishermen, canoeists and hikers.

To reach Bill's take 70 past Hancock; exit left to 68 and go about 13 miles west to exit 68. Turn left off the exit ramp onto Little Orleans Road. Bill's and the canal are about six miles away.

The **Paw Paw Tunnel**, a 3,118-foot brick-lined structure near the western end of the canal, was proclaimed a Wonder of the World when it was built. Canal historian George Hooper Wolfe described it as a "perfect piece of work." The National Park Service calls the tunnel "the largest and most impressive structure on the canal."

Impressive though it may be as an engineering feat, the tunnel also offers a good opportunity to learn about life for the men who blasted through the mountain and other canal laborers who dug the great ditches throughout the Mid-Atlantic. Their work was dangerous, exhausting, unpredictable and poorly paid.

Cost estimates for canal construction and the difficulty of the work were generally pitifully underestimated. For example, initial estimates set the costs of construction for the tunnel at $33,500; the final bill was over $600,000. Lee Montgomery, the principal contractor, thought a worker could bore from 7 to 8 feet a day, but the actual progress was 10 to 12 feet a week. The men paid a heavy price for that miscalculation. Montgomery sometimes was unable to pay them and once hid out in Washington for several months until he was able to raise more money.

Canal work was most often performed by Irish immigrants, who had fled worse deprivation in their native country. As Charles Dickens wrote of the Irish laborer, "Who else would dig and delve and drudge and do domestic work and make canals and roads and execute great lines of internal improvements?" The men lost limbs, their sight and

The brick-lined Paw Paw Tunnel.

even their lives in blasting accidents and worked in constant fear of cave-ins.

The men frequently worked 12-hour days in the summer and from dawn to dusk in the winter. For that back-breaking labor, they were paid wages that ranged from $8-10 a month to $14-16 a month, an increase that came about only after their ranks had been depleted by accidents, death, and other hardships. Pay packets might contain scrip, rather than actual money, or contractors might vanish, leaving workers with no wages whatsoever.

Malaria, yellow fever and typhoid took the lives of laborers on other canals, but cholera was the particular scourge of the C&O Canal. The symptoms were terrifying: spasms, cramps, vomiting, bluish-black skin discoloration and kidney failure. The disease first appeared near Williamsport in the summer of 1832. Five workers died within a few days.

Charles Mercer, president of the canal company, tried to sell his board on the need for hospitals, saying, "If the board but imagine the panic produced by a man's turning black and dying in twenty-four hours in the very room where his comrades are to sleep or to dine, they will readily conceive the utility of separating the sick, dying and dead from the living." He proposed buying planks for bunks, blankets and sacks and "as few and as cheap articles...as possible." Even this minimal effort came at a cost to the workers; they were to pay $.25 a month for the use of the hospital and other medical care.

What the National Park Service euphemistically calls worker unrest was the inevitable result of these conditions. Competing factions of Irish workers battled each other at Williamsport, Md., in 1834. Historian Peter Way challenges the conventional view that the conflict resulted only from ethnic rivalries, writing that workers had good reason to fear that they might be dismissed or go without pay. The men were fighting to control the scarce supply of paid jobs.

The most violent incident took place in 1839, when about 100 armed Irish workers marched from the tunnel area to a work camp for German laborers at Little Orleans, 15 miles down river from the tunnel. They beat the German men, throwing one of them into an open fire. The militia quickly took charge, arresting 30 alleged leaders and destroying the Irish shanties in their work camp. Fourteen men were convicted of charges including riot, robbery, arson and assault with intent to kill. They were jailed and later pardoned in 1840.

To reach the Paw Paw Tunnel from the Beltway near Washington, D.C., take 270 northwest to 70. From 70 at Hancock, take 522 south to Berkeley Springs, West Va. Turn right on 9 and drive 28 miles to the town of Paw Paw. Cross the Potomac River bridge into Maryland to the tunnel sign on the right.

Nathaniel Hawthorne wrote that the water of a canal "causes towns— with their masses of brick and stone, their churches and theaters, their business and hubbub, their luxury and refinement, their gay dames and polished citizens— to spring up." There's no better place to try to visualize this transformation than **Cumberland**, the canal's western terminus. Now a town of 24,000 hoping for an economic miracle, the Maryland's Queen City became a thriving transportation hub when the canal, railroad and National Road arrived during the early 19th century. For the last few decades, however, the area has suffered from declining economic opportunities.

A good headquarters for exploration is the **Inn at Walnut Bottom**, located on Cumberland's oldest street. Nearby Washington Street, now a historic district, was the place to live when the town was in its heyday. Bank presidents, judges, a congressman and newspaper publisher, in addition to the usual cadre of business and other civic leaders had homes on this tree-lined street. A brochure available at the **Western Maryland Train Station** (13 Canal St.) will guide you past these homes, which range in style from Federal through Georgian Revival.

History House, at 218 Washington Street, shows the rewards of the canal's arrival for one family. It was built in 1867 for Josiah Gordon, then president of the C&O Canal, and now has nine period rooms, as well as collections of costumes, rare books and medical instruments. The doors and pews at The First Presbyterian Church, located at 11-15 Washington Street, are made of beautifully carved black walnut. Look for the three original Tiffany stained glass windows of the nearby Emmanual Episcopal Church.

Baltimore Street, the city's main drag, has been turned into a pedestrian mall in an effort to lure people downtown. The effort was only partially successful, but hints of Cumberland's past glory remain. Anchoring one end of the mall, at 44 Baltimore Street, is a three-story building, embellished with arched windows and ornate sculpture, which once housed Gross Brothers Department Store. At the corner of Baltimore and South Liberty Street is a bank building, dating to 1865, with turrets, Spanish-tile roof, Romanesque arches and two carved lions. Look up at the facades of the second and third floors of the buildings for a dazzling display of ornate carvings, cupolas, bay windows and intricate trim.

Cumberland's future appears in a colorful map on the wall of Dick Pfefferkorn's office. He heads up the Canal

CanalFest aims for historical authenticity

Place Authority, the officially sanctioned enterprise to use the town's illustrious past to turn around its failing economy. Projects planned for the next five years include rewatering a section of the canal; creating a pedestrian walkway linking the Western Maryland Train Station with the canal and Potomac River; and developing festival grounds. Their price tag is up to $45 million, but Pfefferkorn and others have already put together an impressive package of federal, state and local funding sources.

CanalFest-Cumberland of 1998 bodes well for anyone worried that the town's past might become a commercial commodity. Pfefferkorn was determined to focus on historical authenticity for the first annual canal festival hosted by the authority. The event offered living history presentations of canal life, period artisans, walking tours led by a canal boat captain and a living history encampment.

But the return home of Mark Baker, a Tony-nominated actor, may be even more encouraging. He commutes from

Intricate carvings in the second story of the restored First National Bank of Maryland.

his apartment in Manhattan's East Village to supervise renovation of the 67-year-old New Embassy Theater, once a favorite venue for Westerns and live performances. Baker's family has owned the downtown building since 1981, when his stepfather bought it to house a drapery shop.

Baker has already enlisted the support of Frances Glendening, Maryland's First Lady, who calls the New Embassy "the theater that could." The 52-year-old actor plans to show classic films and present live theater performances. "We've even commissioned our first play," he says. "It'll be based on the diary of a canal captain."

From Frederick, take 70 west until it meets 40 near Clear Spring or take 40 (scenic route) the entire distance.

Chesapeake and Delaware Canal

The Chesapeake and Delaware Canal is the only lock canal in the United States that has become a major sea level shipping artery and a modern commercial success. Each year, about 15,000 vessels travel through the canal, which is part of the water route between Baltimore and Philadelphia.

The canal's advantages were obvious as early as the 17th century, when Augustine Herman, a surveyor and mapmaker, suggested the route. Only a narrow strip of land separated the Delaware River and the Chesapeake Bay, but the journey by ship around the Delmarva peninsula took 300 miles and required a trip across the stormy Atlantic Ocean. In the mid-1760s, Benjamin Franklin surveyed possible routes across the peninsula. Philadelphia business leaders supported the project in 1788, before work had begun on the most important Pennsylvania canals.

The benefits of the canal would likely be felt in Pennsylvania, rather than in Maryland and Delaware, which the canal would cross. In fact, Baltimore businessmen quick-

ly figured out that the canal could threaten their control of
the trade that was then using the Susquehanna River to
reach their port city.

Work on the canal first began in May of 1804; funds were
exhausted by the end of 1805 and new sources of revenue
were in short supply. The canal was in competition with other
internal improvement projects for Pennsylvania money;
Delaware had few resources and Baltimore leaders were dead
set against providing money for a canal that would threaten
their financial well-being. Canal supporters did the only thing
they could and petitioned Congress for support.

Federal support for internal improvements was a hotly
debated issue at the time on both constitutional and political grounds. Historian Ralph Gray points out that the
Chesapeake and Delaware Canal served as a test case for
the principle involved because of its national importance
and the peculiarity of location that made it more valuable to
states other than those through which it would flow.

The need for a recommendation on federal support to
the project led to Secretary of the Treasury Albert Gallatin's
"Report on Roads and Canals" in 1808. Gallatin recommended that the Chesapeake and Delaware Canal receive federal
funds. However, that historic recommendation was eclipsed
by a more important event: the War of 1812. Congress had
neither funds nor energy to spare for internal improvements.

An energetic Philadelphia businessman, Mathew Carey,
revived the canal effort in 1821 and launched a campaign
that yielded $360,000 in pledges for private support.
Delaware came up with $25,000; Maryland, with twice that
amount and the Pennsylvania legislature committed
$100,000. Congress authorized $300,000 in 1825, 20 years
after receiving the first request for support.

The 14-mile canal went from Newbold's Landing
Harbor (now Delaware City) westward to the Back Creek
branch of the Elk River, near Welch Point. Only four locks
were required to surmount the elevation change of 16 feet,
but the canal ended up with an average cost per mile almost
nine times that of the Erie Canal. The final price tag was
more than $2 million, nearly double the original estimate.

*F*ederal
support for
internal
improvements
was a hotly
debated issue
at the time on
both constitu-
tional and
political
grounds.

Rather than mountainous terrain, engineers faced problems beneath the ground. At the eastern end of the canal, a
stretch of spongy marshland produced constant mudslides.
Even more challenging was an area near Summit, De.,
where a formation of boulders, gravel and sand lay on top of
beds of sand that alternated with clay. Workers dragged bar-
rels full of the matter over a 90-foot hill. Men worked with
pick axes, hand shovels and primitive lifting devices because
of the danger of using explosives in the unstable terrain.

A Zealous Litigator

John Randel, Jr. was a visionary and a troublemaker. In 20th-century
America, he might have found an outlet for his energies by suing
tobacco companies or developing model communities. But, in 19th-
century Delaware, he became a decades-long liability for the
Chesapeake and Delaware Canal Company.

The problems began when Benjamin Wright was appointed the
canal's chief engineer, although Randel's qualifications were equally
good. Randel became the contractor for the eastern end of the canal,

agreeing to a contract provision that gave Wright the authority to serve as "umpire and judge" of his work. If Wright certified to the canal company board that Randel "refuses or unreasonably neglects to prosecute this contract," the board could end the relationship.

Contemporaries of the two men thought that Wright was out to get Randel because of previous friction on the Erie Canal. The chief engineer lowered Randel's pay schedule after the New York engineer had already let subcontracts; delayed certifying completed work and generally made his life difficult. In 1825, Wright forced the board to choose between him and Randel by invoking the termination clause, even though Randel had completed nearly half of his work during the first year of a four-year contract.

Randel sued the canal company for breach of contract and undertook other engineering assignments while the case made its way through the courts. Nearly 10 years later, in 1834, a court in Delaware awarded him slightly more than a quarter of a million dollars. At that time, canal workers made around $12 a month and Charles Mercer, president of the neighboring C&O Canal Company, earned an annual salary of $2,000.

Board members tried to evade payment to Randel by collecting tolls only in Maryland and the company office at Philadelphia, rather than in Delaware, where they could be confiscated. They had again underestimated their adversary. With the support of Delaware authorities, Randel arranged for boat captains to be arrested and placed in jail, until they came up with the toll.

The company managed to get the case as far as the U.S. Supreme Court, where it was dismissed. A court in Maryland affirmed the Delaware decision, stipulating that tolls collected were to be applied to settle Randel's claim. The company admitted defeat and in 1836, finally agreed to pay the full judgement. Both Maryland and Delaware enacted special legislation to guarantee the deal and permit the company to borrow more money. An expanded and more representative board of directors was elected and Randel received full payment.

Randel's windfall enabled him to indulge in "wild, chimerical schemes for self-aggrandizement," according to Maryland historian George Johnston. Actually, some of the engineer's ideas seem remarkably inventive and far-sighted, rather than merely fanciful. He suggested elevated railroads and wrote to John M. Clayton, secretary of state, describing plans for a new city, Morrisania. It would be an extension of New York City with "avenues...200 feet wide, with parks for trees and tasteful shrubbery."

Randel never lost his zest for litigation. He bought property in Maryland, which he named Randalia, and according to Johnston "was seldom without a law suit on hand."

In the canal's peak year, 1872, more than 1.3 million tons of goods were transported through the waterway. The C&D began to lose business in the latter part of the 19th century, but as a transportation route, it maintained a powerful appeal. President Theodore Roosevelt appointed a commission in 1906 to consider conversion of the canal to a sea-level waterway. In 1919, the federal government bought the canal for $2.5 million and made it part of the newly designated Intercoastal Waterway–Delaware River to Chesapeake Bay, Delaware and Maryland

The Army Corps of Engineers began the first of a never-ending series of canal enlargements and improvements. At a cost of $10 million, they removed three of the canal's four locks and converted the waterway to a sea-level operation at 12 feet deep and 90 feet wide. Plans were already underway for a second expansion when the refurbished canal opened in 1927. Between 1935 and 1938, the channel was deepened to 27 feet and widened to 250 feet, at a cost of nearly $13 million. In 1954, Congress authorized expansion to 450 feet wide and 35 feet deep. Work began in the 1960s, but before it was completed the Army Corps of Engineers confronted a new force: the environmental movement.

With $80 million already spent on the project, Congressman Gilbert Gude warned that the enlargement might bring about an environmental disaster. He was concerned about the loss of fresh water from Chesapeake Bay and the impact a change in salinity might have on marine life, particularly oysters. The congressman argued that traditionally research findings had been ignored in favor of new construction, but that now priorities had to be reversed to avoid any more damage to the environment.

At Gude's request, George Fallon, chair of House Committee on Public Works, convened hearings on the canal enlargement in April of 1970. The testimony was a fascinating precursor to the battles between environmental and economic interests that soon would be taking place throughout the entire country. J. Millard Tawes, secretary of the state's Department of Natural Resources, tried to place himself in both camps, by expressing concern about the loss of fresh water from Chesapeake Bay and also advocating greater use of the Port of Baltimore. Representatives of unions and business groups predicted financial hardship if the project were not allowed to go ahead and scientists expressed uncertainty about the impact of enlargement on the environment.

The committee allowed the project to proceed, but the Corps was required to undertake more studies while it was underway. Even more important, Congressman Fallon publicly noted that henceforth the Corps should incorporate environmental concerns in its construction plans.

Just three years after the hearings, the economic importance of the canal was dramatically revealed, when a ship in the canal crashed into a railroad bridge. The Delmarva Peninsula lost its only rail connection to the rest of the country and the canal was shut down. Ships requiring a vertical clearance in excess of 47 feet were forced to sail the outside route between Baltimore and Philadelphia, which added nearly 300 miles to each journey. The Port of Baltimore lost an estimated $1.5 million every day the canal was closed and the loss soon was felt in very human terms. Within a few weeks, about 800 workers in the canal area had been laid off and the jobs of 7,000 more were in danger.

Ralph Gray, the canal's premier historian, wrote in the preface to the second edition of *The National Waterway*,"...it is unlikely that the canal dimensions, a channel width of 450 feet and a depth of 35 feet, will ever be substantially increased, for both economic and environmental reasons."

In 1988, one year before the date of that prediction, however, Congress passed a resolution authorizing the Army

Corps of Engineers "to assess the feasibility of measures to promote and encourage the efficient, economic and logical development of the canal system serving the Port of Baltimore." That lofty language meant that the Corps had the power to undertake studies concerning canal enlargement. A feasibility study was completed in 1996 that recommended deepening the canal to 40 feet.

Much has changed since Gude's initial sounding of an environmental alarm. The feasibility study that recommended canal enlargement is being followed by another study that considers these environmental questions: Will channel modifications raise salinity levels in the canal and adversely affect fish and other aquatic life or contaminate freshwater aquifers? Will increases in shipping traffic cause more oil spills, ballast water discharge, boating accidents or shoreline erosion? Will the disposal of sediments dredged from the channel result in the loss of wildlife habitat or in contamination of area groundwater?

A working group including representatives of civic and environmental organizations is reviewing the study information and bringing the information to interested constituencies.

Chesapeake and Delaware Canal Museum

When it opened in 1968, this small museum was a welcome indication of a changed attitude on the part of the Army Corps of Engineers. In its long series of canal enlargements, the Corps had demolished homes and businesses and had even uprooted and moved bodies from a cemetery. The decision to build and staff the museum was an important gesture of reconciliation.

The immediate impetus for the museum was a campaign by the Cecil County Historical Society to save a historic lift wheel, which raised water from Back Creek and dumped it into a raceway that emptied into the canal. The apparatus was designed to compensate for loss of water in the locks. As boats passed through locks at Chesapeake City, the equivalent of a full lock of water escaped to the lower part of the canal. Two steam engines powered the wheel, which transferred 170 tons of water per minute into the canal.

Henry Ford had tried to buy the piece of machinery and a curator at the Smithsonian praised its historical significance, calling it "the only one of its kind in the country." The society also fought to preserve the iron pumphouse in which the wheel is located.

These historic items were slated for removal, but the Corps agreed to preserve them and build a connecting museum with exhibits that detail the canal's history. The result is a wonderful mixture of the old and new. You'll find a collection of fossils, a display of historic documents, including a list of 19th-century canal tolls and a wall mural depicting the canal in its early years. Immediately to the left of that rendition is a photograph of a modern $60 million bridge built over the canal at St. George, Delaware.

You can watch the progress of a boat through the canal on a computer screen that shows the vessel's rate of speed and estimated time of arrival. Directly beneath the screen is a tangible reminder of the obstacles faced by the early canal laborers: a plain wooden bucket that was used to drag earth up from the canal channel near the Deep Cut. A video

An interactive video traces the canal's history.

gives a very abbreviated version of the canal's history from conception to its modern incarnation.

Maps are a strong suit. At the museum's entrance a large wall map traces both the canal's route and the journey boats were forced to make before the waterway was built. Another map delineates the five canal routes debated by 19th-century engineers.

Look for the working model of the lift waterwheel, which shows how water was pumped into troughs and eventually flowed into the canal. In an adjoining room, the original water wheel and pumping engines are on display.

From Baltimore take route 40 or I-95 to Elkton. Take 213 south to the Chesapeake City Bridge. Cross and follow signs. Open Monday-Saturday 8:00-4:15. 410-885-5622.

Chesapeake City

When canal construction began in 1804, the eastern terminus went by the modest name of Village of Bohemia. By 1850, the canal had brought prosperity to the area and a more imposing designation: Chesapeake City. This era of successful commerce has left a legacy of wonderful 19th-century buildings, which can be seen on a self-guided walking tour. The Victorian-era homes all seem to have front porches; flowers fill the yards and blue water dazzles in the background.

Residents haven't forgotten their canal heritage, however. Canal Artworks at 17 Bohemia St. and the Horn and Hound Fine Arts & Interiors at 98 Bohemia St. both focus on local scenes, including the Chesapeake Bay and canal. Keep walking down Bohemia to the waterfront, where the Pell Gardens offers a beautiful location in which to rest, eat a homemade ice cream cone from the Canal Creamery and gaze out over the canal.

Long-time resident Ralph Hazel (410-885-5088) takes visitors on sightseeing tours of the canal and Chesapeake Bay on his 42-foot boat Miss Clare. He's an expert on local lore. "Did you know that Edna Ferber was inspired by showboats traveling on the C&D to write her famous book?," he asks. He also seems to be able to judge an audience. "Kids sometimes get bored with the history, but they love to see the osprey nests," he says.

Two popular restaurants: Bayard House (11 Bohemia Ave.) and Schaefer's Canal House (208 Bank St.) give visitors a chance to eat seafood while watching boat traffic on the Chesapeake and Delaware Canal. The later restaurant, which is on the shore opposite the canal museum, has been relocated three times to make way for canal enlargements.

`Modern day Chesapeake City shows the scars of its involvement with the canal. In the 1960s, when the canal had been widened and deepened in the Chesapeake City vicinity, not only were 30 to 40 residences and 20 businesses razed, but an underground waterline was excavated and never replaced. The city was permanently divided when the last low-level bridge was replaced by a high-level structure.

Susquehanna Museum of Havre de Grace at the Lockhouse

Like the C&D, the route of the Susquehanna and Tidewater Canal offered tremendous commercial advantages. Although it was only 45 miles long, the waterway opened up all of central Pennsylvania to trade with Philadelphia and Baltimore, by taking advantage of existing transportation connections.

The canal began in Wrightsville, Pa., opposite the Pennsylvania Mainline Canal basin at Columbia, and then traveled 26 miles in Pennsylvania, ultimately ending at Havre de Grace, Md., where the Susquehanna River enters the upper end of the Chesapeake Bay. Canal boats could then cross over the bay, journey through the 14-mile C&D Canal and enter the Delaware River for the trip to Philadelphia or they could travel south from Havre de Grace to Baltimore.

Unfortunately, the canal shared other similarities with the C&D. Sectional loyalties and fear of competition delayed construction for years. Getting the project under-way required cooperation between two states and an uneasy truce between the commercial centers of Baltimore and Philadelphia. Baltimore merchants seemingly had the most to gain and Philadelphia business interests fought the canal, until Pennsylvania state legislators finally gave in to pressure from counties in the Susquehanna Valley.

Work began in 1835 and the canal opened in 1840. To overcome an elevation change of 233 feet, 29 locks were built along the 45-mile route. With canal boats traveling about three miles per hour and encountering a lock about every mile and a half, the trip took a couple of days. The canal enjoyed its most profitable years in the 1870s and was eventually eclipsed by the railroad.

The museum is part of a small complex of restored structures, located at the southern terminus of the canal. It is housed in an 1840 lockhouse facing the river. Two front doors indicate that the building served both as a home for the locktender and an office to collect tolls for north-bound

boat traffic. Imagine a 19th-century garage sale and you'll get the flavor of this lockhouse museum. It contains two floors filled with items like a 100-year-old bicycle with canvas tires, a high chair that converts to a stroller, a Steinway piano and other quirky artifacts of the canal era. A video describes the canal's operation.

A restored lock is directly in front of the lockhouse. A pivot bridge, used for pedestrian and animal traffic across the canal, was reconstructed in 1983. Remains of the wharf to which canal boats were tied are visible at low tide.

Philadelphia Electric Company gave the property to the city of Havre de Grace. Local citizens formed a non-profit organization that operates the museum with support from state and federal grants.

P.O. Box 253, Havre de Grace, 21078 Open Sundays. 1-5 p.m.; April through October. 301-939-5780

Havre de Grace

Havre de Grace, at the southern terminus of the Susquehanna and Tidewater Canal, is filled with attractions related to the water and canal history. Get a copy of the self-guided tour brochure published by the Chamber of Commerce and begin at Tydings Park, which offers beautiful views of the Susquehanna Flats of Chesapeake Bay. Within walking distance is the Decoy Museum, at 215 Giles St., which celebrates the craftsmanship required to create the colorful wooden objects used in duckhunting. Contemporary decoy carvers demonstrate their craft on weekends.

Walk along the boardwalk to the waterfront site of the Maritime Museum. As of 1999, it consists of an exhibit trailer, but a building campaign is underway for a permanent home for exhibits on colonial boatbuilding, the War of 1812 and canal commerce. Continue along the boardwalk to the Concord Point Lighthouse, located at the foot of Lafayette St., where the Susquehanna River becomes the Chesapeake Bay. Built in 1827, it was one of eight lighthouses constructed in connection with the opening of the Chesapeake and Delaware Canal. The lighthouse was in continuous operation for more than 150 years and is open to the public on Sundays from May through October.

More than 800 buildings are part of the Havre de Grace Historic District. The British burned the town during the War of 1812, so few 18th-century buildings remain, but dozens of structures exist from the Canal Era.

From Baltimore, take 40 west to Havre de Grace.

Events

Canal Day

The last Saturday in June, people gather in Pell Gardens of Chesapeake City's historic district to celebrate the canal and eat steamed crabs, crab cakes, pit roast beef and all kinds of pastry. The small town is a low-key art colony and local painters and craftspeople sell their wares. Call 410-885-3466 or 800-CECIL-95.

C&O Canal Days

This long-running Williamsport event is held each year during the last August weekend. Old timers reminisce about canal days; park rangers lead walks along the towpath and musicians recreate the sounds of canal music. A traditional ox roast has turned into a pit beef roast. Call 301-223-9729.

CanalFest

This Cumberland event, which was first held in 1998, is distinguished by its emphasis on historical authenticity. It offers a 19th-century civilian encampment, living history presentations of canal life, period artisans, horse-drawn trolley rides, historic exhibits, walking tours led by a canal boat captain and interpretive bike rides along the canal, as well as nationally recognized bluegrass performers. Call 301-724-3655 for a date and information on attractions.

Heritage Hikes

Twice each year, the C&O Canal Association organizes a day-long event on and near the towpath. Usually more than 100 people turn out for the hikes, which last seven to ten miles.   Dinner is at a church or fire hall and more than compensates for whatever calories have been burned on the trail. The real devotees also show up for monthly short hikes and frequent work parties. Call 301-983-0825.

Organizations

C&O Canal Association,
P.O. Box 366, Glen Echo, MD 20812.
301-983-0825

Tourist Information

Chesapeake and Ohio Canal National Historical Park
PO Box 4, Sharpsburg, MD 21782
301-739-4200
The park has visitors centers at Georgetown in Washington,
D.C.(202-653-5190); Great Falls Tavern in Potomac, Md.
(301-299-3613); Williamsport (301-582-0813); Hancock
(301-722-8226) and Cumberland (301-722-8226).

Havre de Grace Tourism Commission
800-851-7756 or *hdg-tourism.com*

Maryland Office of Tourism Promotion
800-543-1036   *www.mdisfun.org*

Visitor's bureaus, traveling west to east along the canal, are:
Allegany County Visitor's Bureau, Mechanic & Harrison
    Streets, Cumberland 21502. Call 800-508-4748.

Washington County Convention and Visitor's Bureau, 16
    Public Square, Hagerstown 21740. Call 800-228-STAY.

Tourism Council of Frederick County, 19 E. Church St.,
    Frederick, Md. 21701. Call 800-999-3613.

Convention and Visitor's Bureau of Montgomery County,
    12900 Middlebrook Road, Germantown. 20874. Call
    301-428-9702.

Publications

The Canaller, a monthly newsletter published by the National Park Service, describes canal park activities. Available at Great Falls Tavern Visitors Center at 11710 MacArthur Blvd., Potomac, Md 20815 and on the Internet at *nps.gov/choh/co*. Ask at any visitor's center for a free map of the park.

Gray, Ralph D. *The National Waterway: A History of the Chesapeake and Delaware Canal.* Urbana and Chicago, Ill.:University of Illinois Press. 1989
A very detailed, definitive history of the canal.

Gude, Gilbert. *Small Town Destiny: The Story of Five Small Towns along the Potomac Valley.* Mt. Airy, Md., 1989.

Hahn, Thomas. *Towpath Guide to the C&O Canal.* Shepherdstown, West Va.: American Canal and Transportation Center, 1997
This quirky, personal mile-by-mile account of the canal, first published in 1972, offers history, ecology, geology, pictures, maps and the personal reactions of a lifelong canal supporter.

High, Mike. *The C&O Canal Companion.* Baltimore, Md.: Johns Hopkins University Press, 1997.
This guide shows the results of serious historical research, particularly about the Civil War. It has good maps and is well-written and organized.

Kytle, Elizabeth. *Home on the Canal.* Washington, DC: Seven Locks Press, 1983.

Mulligan, Kate. *Towns along the Towpath.* Washington, DC: Wakefield Press, 1997.
A guide to local history, festivals, museums and ways to experience life in canal towns.

Sanderlin, Walter S. *The Great National Project:A History of the Chesapeake and Ohio Canal.* Baltimore, Md. Johns Hopkins University Studies in Historical and Political Science, 1946.

Western Maryland Room of the Washington County Free Library System at 100 South Potomac St., in Hagerstown has a good selection of canal materials and is home to the collected canal papers of Justice William O. Douglas.

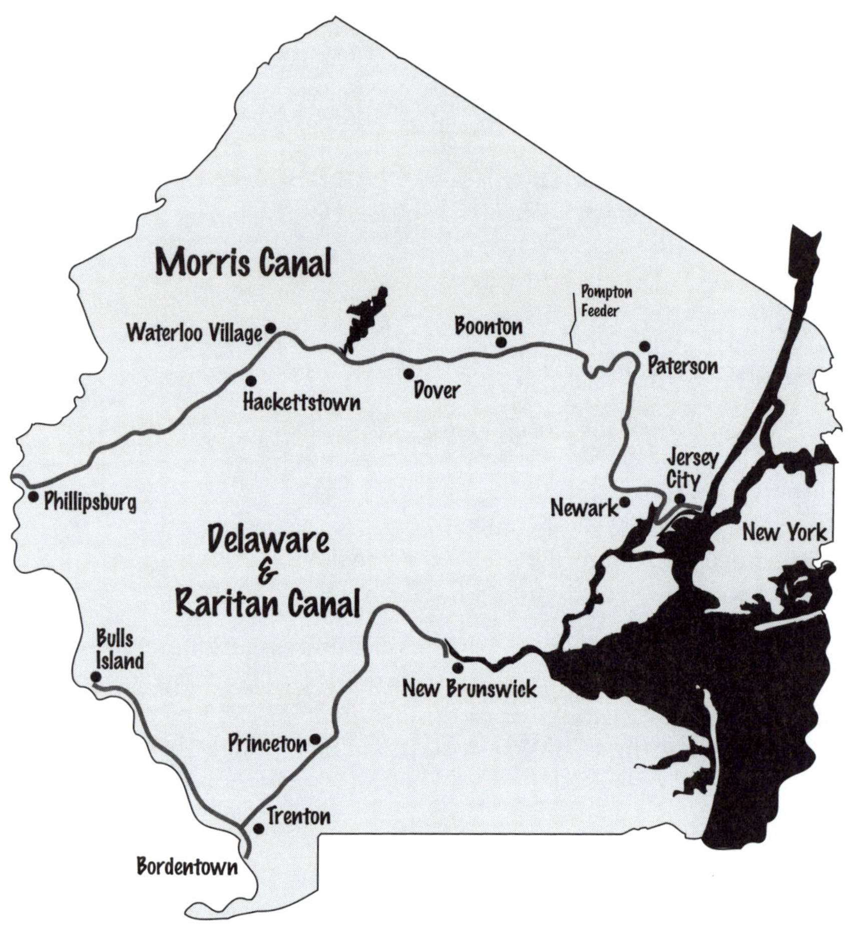

New Jersey ended up with two major canals in the 19th century. Today, canal buffs hunt for remains of the Morris Canal, which was almost completely dismantled by the state. To the south, the Delaware and Raritan Canal is the focal point for a popular park and a water supply.

Nᴇᴡ Jᴇʀsᴇʏ

New Jersey canal builders conquered man-made obstacles like legislative gridlock as well as the more conventional problems of mountainous terrain. They forged unconventional alliances with their usual rivals—railroad companies—and weathered a particularly brazen siege of embezzlement, fraud and mismanagement. As in Pennsylvania, the engineering challenges also stimulated an inspirational display of ingenuity and sheer stubbornness.

The state ended up with two major canals. In 1830, the Morris Canal was completed from Phillipsburg (across from Easton, Pa.) on the Delaware River to Newark on the Passaic River and extended to the Hudson River by 1836. Work began on the Delaware & Raritan Canal in 1831 and was completed in 1834. That canal traveled 44 miles northeast from Bordentown on the Delaware to New Brunswick on the Raritan River. A 22-mile navigable feeder canal brought water from the Delaware to the main canal in Trenton.

Both canals lost battles with railroad transportation, but that's about all their recent histories have in common. The Lehigh Valley Railroad, which leased the Morris Canal in 1871, lobbied for many years for permission to end its canal operation. Company officials viewed the canal as a tax burden and competition with its rail business. When the canal finally was abandoned in 1924, state officials ordered that all canal works be destroyed. Buildings were razed; masonry, destroyed and water drained from the canal bed. An order even went out to dynamite the beautiful stone viaduct that carried the canal over the Passaic River at Little Falls.

The same year the Lehigh Valley Railroad leased the Morris Canal, the Pennsylvania Railroad Company took a 999-year-lease on the Delaware & Raritan Canal and a rail connection across the state. By 1893, the canal was operating at a loss and railroad officials had no interest in making its operation competitive with rail service. The canal closed in 1932 and never reopened. The company turned the canal over to the state three years later.

The Delaware and Raritan Canal played an unexpected role in developing New Jersey's economic strength in the 20th century. Water became a valuable commodity when industrial development spread from urban areas to central New Jersey during the 1930s. In 1944, after several studies, the state began rehabilitating the canal so it could be used as a water conduit. Today, the canal earns the state millions of dollars annually through its sales of water to farms, industry and homes.

The state legislature created the Delaware and Raritan State Park in 1974 and residents now hike and bike along its towpath and canoe in canal waters. In Trenton, city officials are proposing the canal as a major attraction in their efforts to revitalize the city. The D&R is heading into the 21st century as a beloved New Jersey workhorse.

There are few tangible remains of the Morris Canal, but their absence doesn't deter the canal's admirers. In fact, canal historian Joseph Macasek writes, "I am convinced that part of the Morris Canal's allure is due to its elusive nature." He and other canal fans track physical remnants, restore sections of the canal, create small parks, develop exhibits and debate its history. The Canal Society of New Jersey is helping to build a trail that will parallel the canal's route, whenever possible.

New Jersey offers a good mixture of canal attractions. Bike or hike along the D&R Canal towpath for subtle reminders of canal history. Stop at the Mule Tenders Barracks Museum in the historic area of Griggstown, where the local historical society offers canal exhibits or travel to Lambertville, a canal town with appealing 19th-century architecture. Join the members of the Canal Society of New Jersey for one of their regularly scheduled walks and learn about the park from people who know it as well as their own neighborhoods.

At Waterloo Village, near Stanhope, the remains of the Morris Canal are only one of many attractions at a popular tourist destination. Visitors can also explore a recreated Lenape Indian village, listen to a folk concert and watch historical reenactment. The Canal Society of New Jersey operates a museum with canal artifacts, models and a video.

Not far away, at Lake Hopatcong, a museum offers exhibits about the impact of the canal on neighboring areas. Visit the small town of Clifton to admire the work of Jack Kuepfer, who mobilized his neighbors to restore a section of the Morris Canal and create a canal park. You might even meet up with Kuepfer who works in the park a couple of hours each morning when the weather is good.

Delaware and Raritan Canal

William Penn proposed the Delaware and Raritan Canal in 1676. More than 100 years later, in his famous report on internal improvements, Albert Gallatin recommended that the canal's construction receive federal support. For a century, it served as one of America's most successful commercial canals and in 1871, carried more cargo than the longer and more famous Erie Canal ever recorded in a single year. Today, the D&R is the focal point of one of the country's most attractive canal parks.

In the early 19th century, however, it seemed as if the canal might never be dug. Construction was delayed by debate with Pennsylvania over the diversion of water from the Delaware River and then by bickering in the state legislature between interests in the northern and southern parts of the state over the most advantageous canal route. Those delays gave the new-fangled railroad time to gain respectability as a transportation alternative. The state legislature chartered the Camden and Amboy Railroad Company and the Delaware and Raritan Canal Company together as the Joint Companies in 1830.

The state legislature gave the combination a valuable

It carried more cargo than the longer and more famous Erie Canal.

monopoly, stipulating that no other modes of freight transportation could be built in their territory. In return, New Jersey received one thousand shares of stock from each of the companies and a guarantee of $30,000 annually in fees.

When the canal opened in 1834, it seemed destined for success. Construction costs had been low and the work of the canal engineers was excellent. More important, by virtue of the generosity of the legislature, the Joint Companies had a stranglehold on the transportation route that linked Philadelphia and New York, then the two largest cities in the country.

Later, the reach of the canal extended even further. The feeder canal was enlarged and connected with the Delaware River at Lambertville by a lock; on the opposite shore another lock linked the river to the Delaware Canal. Coal could then come down the busy Lehigh Canal to the Delaware Canal, cross the river and proceed to New York first, via the feeder canal and then the main canal. Boats also came up through the Chesapeake and Delaware Canal from the south to the Delaware River and then traveled the main canal to New York.

The Delaware and Raritan Canal should have been a real bonanza for the residents of New Jersey, because the state was a stockholder in the enterprise. But the company issued only sketchy and inaccurate reports about its income and expenditures, enabling it to evade payment of dividends. Several committees of the legislature investigated but did nothing "but apply whitewash," according to historian Alvin Harlow. In fact, in 1854, the legislature extended the monopoly for another 15 years. An observer at the time wrote, "The Company is the paramount authority in the State, dictating legislation upon all subjects in which it has a real or fancied interest."

Corruption didn't stop the Delaware and Raritan Canal from flourishing well into the late 19th century, even though much of its benefit was felt out of the state. Pennsylvania coal headed for New York markets made up most of the tonnage shipped. In 1871, its record year, nearly 3 million tons of goods were shipped on the canal. Ultimately, the canal was closed in 1932 because of competition from railroads.

The Park Bureaucrats

Jim Amon is at the podium to dedicate a new trail segment at Lambertville

Visitors to the Delaware and Raritan Canal State Park owe a special thanks to a couple of government bureaucrats: Eugene Schneider and Jim Amon.

The former was director of an association of county and municipal governments in 1974, when he was enlisted to draft legislation establishing the park. Schneider remembers, "Development was rampant in New Jersey. We saw the chance to promote environmentally sound practices, as well as to preserve green space."

Any successful legislation would have to come up with a good answer to a big question. What kinds of tools would enable an administrator to deal successfully with all the entities that have an interest in the park? The canal runs through 17 municipalities in four counties, each with its own planning and zoning authority and is also subject to decisions taken by state agencies, particularly with regard to the sale of canal water. Often, only a narrow strip of park land separates the canal from private property. It was inevitable that historic preservationists would fight for canal restoration; bicyclists would demand a smooth towpath; environmentalists would insist on unpopulated green space.

The legislation established a new entity, the Delaware and Raritan Canal Commission, to administer the park, rather than placing it within an existing state agency. Its governing body is composed of eight citizen commissioners, with *ex officio* representation from the Department of Environmental Protection. A stipulation that no more than four members be of the same political party protects the agency from politicization. Each of the four counties is represented on the board.

The concept of "review zone" turned out to be even more important to the park's future than its independence. Legislation defined the review zone as an area in which a project, structure, land use change or public improvement requiring municipal approval could have a negative impact on the park and gave the commission the authority to reject, modify or approve any project within the zone.

In practical terms, the legislators handed the commission a valuable tool for use in negotiations with anyone intent on development near the park. The right of review is not absolute, however. The commission judges each proposed project to determine its conformity with a previously developed master plan for the park.

Schneider is delighted with the results of the legislation and gives a great deal of credit to the commission's executive director. "No one is so purely identified with the park as Jim Amon," he says. "He's an unusual bureaucrat who has done a marvelous job."

Amon, a former editor at Oxford University Press, spent time on state environmental issues before accepting the position in 1974. "I thought everything interesting would be done in three or four years," he says. "But I'm still here."

Park advocates think it's lucky Amon hasn't gotten bored and moved on to another challenge. Linda Barth, board member of D&R Canal Watch, says, "Jim works very well with all kinds of groups. He's walked every inch of the canal and is its best salesman."

Numbers give one measure of the park's popularity and his success. Visitation climbed from 5,000 in 1975 to 800,000 in 1998. A more subtle indicator is the fact that Amon has used the negotiating powers inherent in the legislation to get $8 million worth of park improvements made without public expense.

Amon views the park's diverse constituency as an asset, rather than an administrative headache, and says, "The park's greatest advantage is its ability to attract and hold people's affection. In fact, it's a creation of citizen's groups, municipal agencies and county organizations as much as of the state."

Delaware & Raritan Canal State Park

The park includes about 30 miles along the feeder canal from Frenchtown to downtown Trenton and about 34 miles along the main canal from New Brunswick to Trenton. Route 1 covers one mile of the main canal in Trenton and Route 18 covers one mile in New Brunswick.

The towpath along the main canal from Bakers Basin Road to New Brunswick has a natural surface that is good for hiking, biking and horseback riding. The trail along the feeder canal is located on the former right-of-way of the Belvidere-Delaware Railroad and is also suitable for biking.

Visitor's centers are located at Kingston (on route 27),Griggstown (north of route 518) and on Bulls Island, north of Lambertville. Park headquarters is at 625 Canal Road, Somerset 08873. 732-873-3050.

Here are highlights along the feeder canal, traveling southeast from Frenchtown.

A 24-acre natural area is located on the southern portion of the **Bull's Island Recreation Area**. A trail beginning near the park office parallels the canal to the southernmost point of the island and provides views of both the canal and the Delaware River. There are tent and trailer sites at the recreation area.

Walk southeast along the towpath about three miles to reach the **Prallsville Mill** complex. There are nine buildings, whose construction spans a period from 1796 to the early 20th century. The most prominent building, the grist mill built in 1877, is a four-story masonry building that is used for exhibits, concerts, and community events. The Wickecheoke Creek flows into the canal, which has a long spillway into the Delaware River.

Entrance to Bull's Island is about 3 miles northwest of Stockton on Route 29. 2185 Daniel Bray Highway, Stockton 08559. 609-397-2949.

For a sense of rural life during the 19th century, visit the **Holcombe-Jimison Farmstead Museum**, which is operated by the Hunterdon County Historical Society. On display are farming equipment, a farm kitchen, country doctor's office, country post office and other farm-related items. The farm is about three miles from the Prallsville complex.

1605 Daniel Bray Highway, Lambertville 08530. Open Sundays from 1-4 p.m. from May to October. 609-397-2752

Almost the entire city of **Lambertville** is designated as a national registered Historic District. Most of the houses, shops and abandoned factories that adjoin the Delaware & Raritan Canal are 19th-century structures. Not surprisingly, the area has become an antiques mecca, with more than 40 shops and design centers. It also is home to an excellent selection of bookstores, including two—Phoenix Books and Left Bank Books—that specialize in first editions and other rare books.

The canal itself is nicely represented by two locks, several bridges, two aqueducts, a beautiful stone arched culvert, a locktender's house and a good stretch of towpath. Access to the towpath is via a short stretch of gravel road

Prallsville Mill

leading from the rear of the parking lot at the Lambertville
Station Restaurant.

The town is famous for the Shad Festival, which is held
each year during the last April weekend. The two-day arts
and crafts event celebrates the return of the shad to the
upper Delaware River. Check out the Marshall House
Museum, 62 Bridge St., open from 1-4 the last weekend of
each month from April to October. The museum is operated
by the Lambertville Historical Society, which offers guided
walking tours. The Chamber of Commerce (609-397-0055)
has a brochure for a self-guided walking tour that includes
the home of the canal's chief engineer.

Park officials have big plans for Lambertville. They envision a canal boat ride that begins south of the town and
travels through a restored canal lock and also plan to
rebuild the outlet lock to the Delaware River so that ferry
service to New Hope can be restored.

Washington Crossing State Park is best known as the
site on which George Washington landed on December 25,
1776, prior to his march to Trenton, 10 miles away. His victory at the Battle of Trenton was a crucial episode in the
struggle for American independence. The most visible
reminder of canal history is the Alexander Nelson House,
which served canal boatmen before it become a hotel for
commercial travelers in the Victorian era. The house was
renovated in 1980 by the Washington Crossing Association
of New Jersey to serve as a center for historical displays.
The park has 13 miles of hiking trails, picnic facilities and
opportunities for fishing.

Located at the juncture point of the main and feeder
canals, **Trenton** was a big winner when the D&R finally
opened for business. Canal traffic stimulated the growth of
ironworks, ceramic factories and other businesses, and the
city's population increased four-fold within a few years.

Its more recent history has not been as fortunate. In
places, the main canal was filled in; at one point, it disap-
pears under route 1. Canal turning basins were also filled in
and historic swing bridges replaced with concrete structures
that are too low to allow canoes to pass.

Alan Malloch, head of planning and redevelopment for Trenton, is optimistic about the area's potential and thinks the canal can be an important asset in revitalization efforts. He's looking forward to the day when new housing will attract residents back to this historic downtown area. "About 500 feet from the towpath is a beautiful 19th-century building which now serves as the city museum for Trenton. It's in Cadwalader Park, which was designed by Frederick Olmstead of Central Park fame," he says. A 150-foot monument commemorating the Battle of Trenton is also close to the towpath.

The towpath passes a few blocks from the historic state capitol and the Old Barracks Museum, which housed troops during both the French and Indian and Revolutionary Wars and now offers frequent living history events.

Here are highlights of the main canal, traveling northeast.

Calling it "a little town with a big history," *New Jerseytimes*, a public radio series, highlighted **Bordentown**, south of Trenton, on a show featuring canal towns. The commentators came up with a fascinating assortment of historical tidbits. Clara Barton, who went on to found the American Red Cross, taught school here and helped launch the public school movement in New Jersey. Joseph Bonaparte, King of Spain and Napoleon's older brother, fled to Bordentown after the Battle of Waterloo and filled a mansion with jewels and treasures. The building was demolished by a subsequent owner to demonstrate his hatred of tyranny, but an elegant gate house remains to remind residents of all that splendor. The considerably less flamboyant Thomas Paine, author of *Common Sense*, also spent several years in Bordentown. Check with the Bordentown Historical Society at 609-298-1740 for information about exhibits at the Gilder House Museum.

Head for Turning Basin Park at 493 Alexander Road in **Princeton** to rent canoes for travel on the canal. The Historical Society of Princeton at 158 Nassau St. offers exhibits depicting events from the 18th century to the present and guided tours of the city. Princeton Battlefield State Park at 500 Mercer Road commemorates another important victory of Washington's troops over the British.

The **Mule Tenders Barracks Museum** has a modest name, but a fascinating history. It first housed Irish workers who came to work on the D&R Canal and later offered a night's accommodations to the canal's mule tenders who found the location a good place to change mules for the next stage of their journey.

A beautiful stained glass window is the idiosyncratic addition of a 20th-century owner. The building has also been used as a post office, general store, library, nursery school and living quarters for a whole series of families. It now houses a canal museum and information center, operated by the Griggstown Historical Society.

The Griggstown Historic District stretches for five miles along the eastern end of the park. The Griggstown lock, with an interesting remnant of the bypass channel still visible, is in the southern part of the district. At the northern end is the Ten Mile Run culvert, one of the most impressive of the structures designed to take streams under the canal. The district includes 18th- and 19th-century farmsteads, in addition to the canal-related structures. Canoes can be rented.

From New Brunswick, take Route 514 west to East Millstone and take Canal Road south. The museum is located on the Griggstown Causeway, which stretches between Canal and River Roads.

Morris Canal

In 1832, British author Frances Trollope called the Morris Canal "an extraordinary work." In a recent radio interview, Rutgers professor Michael Rockland labeled it a real Rube Goldberg operation, adding, "The whole Morris Canal is incomprehensible to us...because we can't quite believe that anyone would go to that much trouble to build that canal."

Both observers were correct—the canal was extraordinary and also a great deal of trouble. In its 102- mile length, it conquered a rise and fall that totaled nearly 1,700 feet. It climbed 914 feet from sea level at Jersey City to reach Lake Hopatcong, its primary water source, and then dropped 760 feet as it traveled west to Phillipsburg.

The Erie Canal, by contrast, overcame an elevation change of 700 feet in the course of 363 miles, using 77 locks in the process, and the Panama Canal rose only 85 feet in 50 miles. When engineers for the Pennsylvania Mainline Canal finally confronted the intractable Allegheny Mountain, they temporarily abandoned canal construction and built a railroad over the obstacle.

Engineers first planned to use the conventional method of overcoming change in elevation: a system of canal locks. But calculations showed that 200 locks would be required to get boats from one end of the canal to the other. They then turned to a solution that made the canal famous: the inclined plane.

The name of James Renwick, the country's most celebrated engineer, usually is linked with the inclined plane, but canal promoter George P. Macculloch attributed its invention to Robert Fulton and gave Renwick credit for adapting the plane for use on the canal. Neither man mentioned an Englishman named Fussell, who had patented a similar invention more than 20 years earlier.

The basic task was simple: to move a canal boat up an inclined plane from one level to the next. A canal boat floated into a cradle car, which rode on iron rails that were much like railroad tracks. Water from the upper section of the canal flowed through a pipe down to an underground turbine. The force of the water powered the turbine, enabling a cable to pull the cradle and boat up the incline. The completed canal used 23 locks and 23 inclined planes, with the highest plane overcoming an elevation of 100 feet.

The Morris Canal was an uneasy triumph over political squabbles and sectionalism, as well as elevation. George P. Macculloch, a Morristown businessman, found himself in an ideal position to promote the interests of northern New Jersey when he was appointed by the state legislature to a commission that would recommend a canal route. But his proposed route was challenged by John Rutherford, who supported the Delaware and Raritan Canal, which would promote economic development in Trenton and New Brunswick.

In 1824, the state legislature broke the gridlock by finessing the issue of where to allocate financial support. Legislators chartered the Morris Canal and Banking Company to build the canal across northern New Jersey. The private company was authorized to sell $1 million worth of stock, but it received no public money. Instead, as a banking company, it had legal authority to issue its own currency, as did other banks at that time.

Macculloch had promoted the canal because he was interested in economic development for his home state. But the charter that was finally approved permitted residents of New York to serve on the board of directors. It also stipulated that directors were to be elected by stockholders, rather than appointed by the legislature.

In today's world of global economics, opening the board to out-of-state residents and to stockholder influence seems a tame gesture. At the time, however, the provisions made the company a target for stock speculators. A newspaper reporter of the time wrote, "The Wall Street bees, attracted by the savor of New Jersey honey, are buzzing around the State House."

Macculloch was furious. The charter stipulated that he would be a director, a position he happily accepted until he learned about the changes that benefitted New York financiers. Here is his reaction, as expressed in a letter to Cadwallader Colden, who later became a company president.

"The precarious position of a canal coupled to a bank and directed by men of operations exclusively financial was obvious. The interests of the country and the development of the iron manufacture were merged in reckless stock speculation. I found myself a mere cipher, standing alone and responsible in public opinion for acts of extravagant folly, which I alone had strenuously opposed at the board of directors...I clung to the sinking ship until every hope of safety had vanished, and then vacated my seat by selling out, thus saving myself from ruin, if not from loss."

Even the indignant Macculloch didn't anticipate all the financial scandals that would plague the canal. They started with the first stock subscription. A down payment of $10 was all that was needed to buy one share on the installment plan. According to historian Barbara Kalata, "The charter authorized the issuing of stock worth $1 million at $100 a share; $7 million was subscribed during the frenzied buying at Jersey City."

By 1826, Macculloch's fears about New York financiers were being realized. Director Henry Eckford "temporarily borrowed" Morris Canal stock worth $250,000 to save his own company, the Life and Fire Insurance Company of New York. Eckford and three other company directors were indicted for conspiracy to defraud. The New Yorker returned the stock; the men were never convicted, but public confidence in the canal was shaken.

More chicanery was to come. Company officials got involved in speculative stock ventures and used company funds to finance their own commercial ventures. In 1837, a year in which banks and businesses were falling like a chain of dominoes, an employee absconded with more than $100,000 in funds. Later, Edward Biddle, who had become company president, mortgaged the canal to the state of Indiana to raise funds that masked the canal company's financial plight. (Indiana actually received a second mortgage. The canal had already been mortgaged to Dutch financial interests.)

By 1841, even the acquiescent board of director had had enough. Biddle and Edwin Lord, vice president of the company, were asked to resign. When they refused, the board appointed a committee to investigate mismanagement of company funds. Their report documented numerous instances of misuse of funds, conflict of interest and unethical behavior.

The Dutch investors called in the mortgage and the canal was sold in 1844. Indiana lost $2.5 million from its ill-fated investment—a loss that sidetracked its own canal-building efforts. But the New Jersey waterway benefited from its brush with disaster. A new company was formed that tackled one of the canal's most serious flaws: its size. The canal was only 31 feet wide and its 75-foot by 9-foot locks could not accommodate boats of more than 25 tons. It was too small for boats used on the Lehigh Canal, where its coal traffic originated.

William Talcott redesigned the inclined plane so that boats carrying 70 tons of coal traveled down the canal. The cost of the modifications came to more than $6 million, but the canal finally showed a profit. In 1845, its coal tonnage was only 58,279; by 1860, it was 707,631 and in 1866, the Morris Canal carried nearly 900,000 tons of cargo.

Even the last chapter of the canal's history was filled with dramatic events and colorful characters. Read below about Hudson Maxim, a millionaire inventor who fought for the canal's abandonment.

An Independent Thinker

Hudson Maxim, a New Jersey inventor, once reported that he had slept badly "because in my dreams I worked all night with a truck filling the Morris Canal." Maxim eventually got his way by bullying the state legislature into releasing the Lehigh Valley Railroad from its contractual obligation to continue operating the canal.

It's hard to get a precise fix on the source of Maxim's animus towards the canal by reading his many tracts. There's no doubt the millionaire was worried about the future of Lake Hopatcong, which supplied the canal with water, but Maxim's logic often gets lost in his invective.

No matter. Maxim was a wonderful Horatio Alger character. Young Hudson was 13 before he owned a pair of shoes, but he had amassed a fortune by the time he was 35. Maxim and his partner Alden Knowles published a highly successful instruction guide to penmanship and later sold more than one million copies of a family record book.

When the introduction of the typewriter ended his publishing business, Maxim moved to England to work in his brother Hiram's gun factory. The young inventor figured out the composition of smokeless gunpowder by studying a French prototype and when he was back in the United States, took out patents on a variety of inventions related to explosives. In 1901, the government awarded Maxim $50,000 for Maximite, an explosive that was 50 percent more powerful than dynamite.

The Du Pont Company built a laboratory for Maxim at Lake Hopatcong. "I came primarily that I might have room to blow up the country without too much interference with neighbors," he told his biographer Clifton Johnson. Maxim turned his attention to torpedoes and invented devices to increase their power.

Johnson quotes a psychologist's view of Maxim's personality. "I never before met a man who combines so perfectly the essentials of a scientific intelligence, and those elemental qualities of strength, candor, and directness of character that are almost as primitive as the forces of nature. He is a veritable 'cave man,' who has stepped forth from an age when the world was young and unconventional."

Read some of Maxim's pronouncements, and you might start to believe that assessment. Take his views about the Spanish American War, for example. He insisted, "The Spanish War impressed me as the ploy of a great braggadocio of a bully, on the part of the United States, hopping on to a little bit of a geezer. It was foolish and stupid and unnecessary to the last degree. The war taught not much more than a battle between two boys armed with peashooters would teach." Strong words for a man who was a close friend of Theodore Roosevelt and also an inventor of weapons.

Most endearing, perhaps, are Maxim's thoughts on women. "Men used to have a much smaller idea of woman as an intellectual potentiality. We used to tell her to mind her knitting, and we did what we could to ensmall her sphere and keep it small. She pleased us better in her primitive innocence, because then we looked big to her, without really being so." This unconventional man even put his views into practice, by giving his wife joint ownership in his bank account and property.

At age 70, Maxim issued this challenge, which gives a good indication of his approach to life. "Activity and useful service are regenerative and constructive. Let any man follow me for a month and he is going to be weary."

Across the Delaware River from Easton, Pa., **Phillipsburg** was the western terminus of the Morris Canal. As of 1999, it is also the location of a very energetic effort to gain state designation as the site for the proposed New Jersey Railroad and Transportation Center. Proponents point to its rich transportation history and cite a 15.5-mile scenic railroad from Phillipsburg to Milford and the area's scenic beauty as current attractions.

A ferry crossed the Delaware beginning in 1739; the

New Brunswick Turnpike opened in 1802 and the Morris
Turnpike in 1806. Between 1829 and 1843, Phillipsburg and
Easton were the junction points of three canals: Lehigh,
Delaware and Morris. By mid-century, almost one-third of
the country's iron was made in the area. The proposed site
includes Delaware River Park, which had a large canal basin
with loading docks for coal. Interpretive signs in the park
explain the importance of the western terminus.

Historic Waterloo Village contains the best collection of
sites related to the Morris Canal. Get a copy of the one-
page handout by the Canal Society of New Jersey, which
offers an annotated map with descriptions of the canal-related remains. Walk along a water-filled section of the canal to
Smith's General Store, where canallers stopped for groceries.
Nearby are remains of a combination lock and aqueduct and
a reconstructed mule bridge. The well-preserved remains of
Inclined Plane 4 are a highlight of the canal walking tour.
The 1825 Rutan Farmsite conveys what life was like for
rural families during the canal era.

Visit the museum operated by the Canal Society of New
Jersey to see what the Morris Canal looked like in the 19th
century. A 15-minute video shows film footage of a towpath

*Lock of Morris
Canal at Waterloo
Village*

canal in operation. The museum also has photographs, drawings, working models and various canal artifacts.

In addition to the canal-related sites, the historic complex offers a re-created Indian Village with huts, longhouses and dugout canoes, representing the Lenape way of life in 1625. From May to October, there is a program of orchestral and chamber concerts, opera, jazz and popular music.

The Canal Society of New Jersey has joined forces with the New Jersey State Parks Department to develop the Morris Canal Greenway, a hiking trail along the route of the canal, and in 1996 opened the Waterloo Valley Section, which is 2.5 miles long. To reach that section, take route 80 to Stanhope, go one mile past Waterloo Village to Kinney Road, which is the first road on the left. The trail is on the side of the bridge closer to Waterloo Road.

Take route 80 to exit 25 and follow signs. 525 Waterloo Road, Stanhope 07874. The village, which is located in Allamuchy Mountain State Park, is open Wed.-Sun., mid-April to mid-November. Admission. 973-347-0900.

Lake Hopatcong provided the lifeblood for the Morris Canal: its water. The canal company joined two lakes, built a dam that raised the level of the water five feet and linked the enlarged lake to the canal with a feeder canal. The lake is now the focal point of an attractive state park.

At the edge of the parking lot near the dam, a turbine wheel from one of the two inclined planes at Ledgewood is on display. The **Lake Hopatcong Historical Museum**, operated by the Lake Hopatcong Historical Society, is located in a locktender's house. The exhibits celebrate the lake's history as a popular summer resort and depict the transformation brought by the Morris Canal. They also tell the tale of Hudson Maxim, the bete noire of canal fans, who advocated the dismantling of the Morris Canal.

The museum is in Lake Hopatcong State Park. Take exit 28 from route 80 west. Open on Sundays from noon to 4:00, March-May and September-November. PO Box 668, Landing 07850. 973-398-2616.

Boonton is a small canal town not far from Paterson, but it's miles away in spirit. During the canal's heyday, hundreds of local residents were employed at the New Jersey Iron Company's Boonton Ironworks, and the town became the largest producer of nails in the country. The bases of two iron furnaces can be seen, although the factory buildings are long gone. Nearby, the aptly named Plane Street is the site of one of the Morris Canal's inclined planes. A towpath trail stretches beside a short stretch of water-filled canal, behind the Boonton Water Supply building. Today, Boonton lays claim to another superlative: site of the largest concentration of antique shops in Morris County.

Take route I-287 north to exit 44. Most of the canal-related sites are on or near Main Street.

From coal mine to foundry, the iron industry was closely linked to canal building. The **Historic Speedwell National Historic Landmark** is the site of the Speedwell Iron Works, an early 19th-century foundry that improbably played a role in Samuel Morse's invention of the telegraph. Alfred Vail, son of the foundry's owner, Stephen Vail, was able to support Morse's activities because of the elder Vail's financial largesse. Morse worked on the telegraph at the Speedwell family estate, Hopewell Farm, and sent his first messages to his benefactor. Of interest to students of the canal era is a special permanent exhibit, "The Speedwell Ironworks: A History of Workers and Work," which shows what's involved in producing iron machinery and how iron workers and their families contributed to the company's growth.

From Boonton, take route 202 south. 333 Speedwell Ave., Morristown 07960. Admission.

Located in the Historic District of Morristown, the building in which the **Macculloch Hall Historical Museum** is housed was home to five generations of the descendants of George P. Macculloch, the legendary promoter of the Morris Canal.

Macculloch Hall, a Federal brick mansion constructed in 1810, is surrounded by 19th-century gardens. Holdings include the archives of the Macculloch family, but the museum's primary strengths are in areas far removed from the gritty struggles of canal building. The museum has more than 2,000 cartoons by Thomas Nast, an extensive collection of oriental carpets and a wide variety of 18th- and 19th-century decorative and fine arts.

Take exit 36 from I-287. From the south, turn left at the end of the ramp onto South Street. Proceed west to Miller Road. Turn left, proceed 2 blocks and turn right onto Macculloch Ave. 45 Macculloch Avenue. Morristown 07960. Admission. 973-538-2404.

Canals often were built with pick and shovel, by Irish laborers who found that even 12-hour days of back-breaking work were preferable to the economic devastation in their native country. **The Museum of Early Trades and Crafts** offers a hands-on view of the past as it traces the legacy of artisans who worked with their hands.

Main Street at Green Village Road. Madison 07940. Closed Mondays. 973-377-2982.

In 1986, Jack Kuepfer, under the auspices of the Clifton Historical Commission, approached the city council with a plan for canal restoration, using volunteer labor. Officials agreed to lease the land for the **Morris Canal Park and Nature Preserve** from the New Jersey Highway Authority and Public Service Electric & Gas Company. Eagle Scouts constructed the canal dam that got the effort underway and have since completed more than 40 other projects. The park contains a restored and watered section of the canal and picnic area.

Kuepfer still comes to the park for a couple of hours every morning when the weather is good. He plants trees each fall and stocks the canal water with a variety of fish. A local contractor regularly digs silt from the canal bed and other volunteers rake leaves, plant flowers and help with carpentry.

From route 3 eastbound, exit on Broad St. Make left at light onto Broad St. Park is on the right.

A Canal Storyteller

"I got in the game early," says Jim Lee. He was only a sophomore in high school when he started talking to canal boatmen who had lost their jobs when the Morris Canal closed. "They were kicked off the canal. Nobody would hire them. I resolved early in life that I'd perpetuate the memory of what they did."

Lee grew up in Port Delaware (now Phillipsburg) at the western terminus of the canal. He remembers floating a hand-made raft in the canal basin, marveling at the coal chutes and visiting the canal office.

World War II temporarily diverted Lee from his obsession. But upon returning from service, he bought the plane tender's house at Plane 9 West near Stewartsville and with the help of his wife, Mary, restored the structure. Lee then unearthed and restored the turbine used to power the inclined plane, when the canal was operating. It had been buried under tons of rock when the canal was abandoned.

While making a living as a railroader, Lee built a collection of canal memorabilia and artifacts. Postcards became a particular passion; he has hundreds of them. "People might not have phones. They'd announce their travel plans on postcards with illustrations of the canal," he says.

"People make history. Machines don't make history," Lee proclaims. Despite his painstaking work with the turbine, Lee's heart remained with the canal boatmen and he set about collecting their stories. The New Jersey Historical Commission gave Lee a small grant to complete the oral histories, and he published *Tales the Boatmen Told* in 1977.

Lee took his slide show on the road for many years. His oral histories were the basis of "Famous Tiller Sharks," a show produced by New Jersey's public television station. Bernard Bush, then executive director of the New Jersey Historical Commission, proclaimed that Lee's historical activities would rival those of a well-staffed and well-funded organization.

Events

Waterloo Canal Day

On the second Saturday in June, members of the Canal
Society of New Jersey present Waterloo's history as a
canal town. Canal tours, talks and even canal beer are
available. Call 908-722-9556 or visit the website at
www.canalsocietynj.org.

Delaware & Raritan Canal Walks

The society hosts 3- to 5-mile walks along the towpath,
with historical interpretation. Call number listed above.

Organizations

Bicycle Advocate
New Jersey Department of Transportation
1035 Parkway Ave.
CN 600
Trenton, NJ 08625

Canal Society of New Jersey
P.O. Box 737
Morristown, NJ 07960
908-722-9556
www.canalsocietynj.org
The society hosts speakers and offers field trips, frequently
to European canals. It offers a brochure containing an
excellent map of New Jersey canals.

Captain Bill McKelvey
103 Dogwood Lane
Berkeley Heights, New Jersey 07922
908-464-9335
Capt. McKelvey offers a series of canal tours and frequently
lectures on canal topics. He's an excellent source for canal
books, including out of print and rare items.

Delaware and Raritan Canal Commission
P.O. Box 539
Stockton, NJ 08559-0539
609-397-2000

D&R Canal Watch
609-924-2683

The Morris County Heritage Commission
Court House P.O. Box 900
Morristown, NJ 07963
201-829-8117

Tourist Information

Delaware River Regional Tourism Council
One Riverside Drive
Camden, NJ 08103
609-365-3300 Ext. 230

Historic Morris Visitor Center
Court St.
Morristown, NJ 07832
973-631-5151

New Jersey Division of Travel & Tourism
PO Box 826
20 West State St.
Trenton, NJ 08625
800-JERSEY 7
http://www.state.nj.us/travel

Publications

Cawley, James and Margaret. *Along the Delaware and Raritan Canal.*
Cranbury, N.J.: Associated University Presses, Inc. 1970.

Davison, Betty. *The Delaware and Raritan Canal: A User's Guide.* Princeton: Delaware and Raritan Canal Coalition, Inc. 1976.

Delaware and Raritan Canal State Park Master Plan.
(Second edition). Stockton, NJ: Delaware and Raritan
Canal Commission. 1989.

Kalata, Barbara N. *A Hundred Years, A Hundred Miles: New
Jersey's Morris Canal.* Morristown: 1983. This book is like a
cabinet full of misfiled material. There's lots of interesting
information, but it takes digging to find it.

Lee, James. *The Morris Canal: A Photographic History.*
Easton, Pa: Canal Press. 1977. The best collection available
of pictures of the Morris Canal.

Lee, James. *Tales the Boatmen Told: Recollections of the Morris
Canal.* Exton, Pa.: Delaware Press. 1979. Wonderful inter-
views with canal captains, drivers, lock and plane tenders
and others associated with the canal.

Macasek, Joseph J. *Guide to the Morris Canal in Morris
County.* (Second edition) Morristown: Morris County
Heritage Commission. 1997. This guide has good maps, pic-
tures and illustrations of canal features. It looks terrific.
The author is at work on a similar guide for Warren County.

McKelvey, William J., Jr.. *The Delaware & Raritan Canal: A
Pictorial History.* York: Pennsylvania Canal Press, Inc. 1975.

Mitros, David. *Directory of Historic Morris County, New
Jersey. A Guide to Historical Resources, Museums, Associations
and Archives.* Morristown: Morris County Heritage
Commission. 1995. Excellent bibliography.

New Jersey Cultural & Historic Guide. Trenton: New Jersey
Division of Travel & Tourism. No date.

RESOURCES

Organizations

American Canal Society
c/o Charles W. Derr, Secretary-Treasurer
117 Main St.
Freemansburg, PA 18017
Membership is $15, which includes a subscription to
American Canals .
blacksheep.org/canals/ACS

National Trust for Historic Preservation
1785 Massachusetts Ave., NW
Washington, D.C. 20036
202-588-6000

Rails-to-Trails Conservancy
1100 17th Street, NW, 10th Floor
Washington, DC 20036
202-331-9696
railstrails.org
This organization worked with the National Park Service to
produce a useful study and fact sheets about developing
canal parks.

Publications

Drago, Harry Sinclair. *Canal Days in America: The History and Romance of Old Towpaths and Waterways*. New York:C.N. Potter. 1972.

Economic Impacts of Protecting Rivers, Trails and Greenway Corridors. Washington, D.C.: Rivers, Trails and Conservation Program of National Park Service. 1995. This study provides useful ammunition for anyone trying to develop a canal park.

Harlow, Alvin. *Old Towpaths: The Story of the American Canal Era*. Port Washington, N.Y.:Kennikat Press. 1964. Harlow is the kind of author you want to call up on the telephone for a chat. He makes no effort to restrain his passions. "The childish obsession speed! —speed!— more speed! had hastened the downfall of the canals," he writes indignantly. The author, who died in 1963, wrote for such publications as the *Saturday Evening Post*, the *New Yorker* and *Colliers*, while making a living in advertising and business. His eclectic interests are reflected in the books he authored, including the intriguely titled *Murders Not Quite Solved*.

Shaw, Robert E. *Canals for a Nation*. Lexington: University Press of Kentucky. 1990. *The Journal of American History* called this book, "The best comprehensive treatment of the canal era available." The book is very readable and has an excellent bibliographical essay.

Towpaths-to-Trails. Washington, D.C.: Rails-to-Trails Conservancy and National Park Service. 1995. A report on the results of a survey about "current conditions of historic canal corridors, their ownership, trail development efforts and obstacles encountered as a result of those efforts."

Way, Peter. *Common Labor: Workers and the Digging of North American Canals 1780-1860*. Baltimore, Md.: Johns Hopkins University Press. 1997.

Zimmerman, Albert G. *Canal Bibliography with a primary emphasis on the United States and Canada*. Easton: Canal History and Technology Press. 1991. Canal scholar Zip

Zimmerman has performed a valuable service by putting together this 187-page publication, which includes more than 2,000 listings.

The Parks and History Association, which sells material on sites in Maryland, can be reached at 800-990-PARK or *ParkStore.com*. Eastern National, which sells material on sites in Pennsylvania and other Mid-Atlantic areas, can be reached at *nationalparkbooks.org*. The National Canal Museum has an online store at *canals.org*. An excellent source for out-of-print books on canal history is *abebooks.com*.

OTHER CANAL PARKS

Augusta Canal National Heritage Area
P.O. Box 2367
Augusta, GA 30903
888-659-8926
augustacanal.com

The 9-mile-long Augusta Canal, which parallels the
Savannah River, was first built in 1845 and enlarged in 1852
and 1875. Today, the canal remains part of Augusta's water
supply system and also supplies hydropower to textile mills.
In 1989, the Georgia Legislature created the Augusta Canal
Authority, which produced a master plan in 1993. Planners
envision a river front park, environmental learning center,
restoration of an 1845 lock and headgates to provide a
venue for a Petersburg boat fleet, kayak run and numerous
other efforts to interpret the area's history. The project got
a boost in 1996 when Congress designated the Augusta
Canal National Heritage Area.

Blackstone River Valley National Heritage Corridor
One Depot Square
Woonsocket, RI 02895
401-762-0440
nps/gov/blac

This linear park, which was designated a national corridor
in 1986, follows the Blackstone River from Providence in
Rhode Island to Worcester in central Massachusetts. The
45-mile Blackstone Canal, which opened in 1828, parallels
the river. Visitors can walk along restored sections of the

canal, leaving from the River Bend Farm Visitor's Center, near Uxbridge, Mass.

Illinois and Michigan Canal National Heritage Corridor
15701 South Independence Blvd.
Lockport, IL 60441
815-740-2047
nps.gov/ilmi

The 96-mile Illinois and Michigan Canal provided the first complete water route from the east coast to the Gulf of Mexico by connecting Lake Michigan to the Mississippi River by way of the Illinois River. In the 1960s, long after the canal had ceased operation, Illinois state officials assessed the value of the property in preparation for selling parcels of land. Public protest stopped the sale and canal supporters helped create a 61-mile I&M Canal State Park from Joliet to LaSalle. In 1984, Congress designated the canal park and some 40 additional miles as the first national heritage corridor. The corridor includes over 40 cities and towns, portions of five counties and nearly 20 Chicago neighborhoods.

Lowell National Historic Park
67 Kirk Street
Lowell, MA 01852
978-970-5000
nps.gov/lowe

Best known for its contribution to the beginning of America's Industrial Revolution, Lowell also played an important role in promoting canal restoration. It was the first site to demonstrate that canal history could have a con-temporary economic payoff. The compact park offers nearly six miles of a restored canal system, the Boott Cotton Mills Museum, the Suffolk Mill Turbine Exhibit and an award-winning video about Lowell's history. Rangers lead a variety of boat tours on the Pawtucket Canal and Merrimack River. Canal Heritage Weekend takes place each fall.

New York State Canal Corporation
P.O. Box 189
Albany, NY 12201
800-4CANAL4
canals.state.ny.us

The home state for the 363-mile Erie Canal is a paradise for today's canal fans. In addition to the Erie, the New York State Canal System includes the Champlain, Oswego and Cayuga-Seneca Canals. Together, they contain more than 500 miles of navigable waterway. Visitors can rent canal boats or join a trip sponsored by a commercial outfitter. Canal-related museums are located at Syracuse, Canastota, Chittenango, Lockport and numerous other towns. The 220-mile Canalway Trail offers opportunities for hiking, bicycling and cross-country skiing. Canal festivals take place almost every weekend during the spring and summer.

Ohio and Erie Canal National Heritage Corridor
P.O. Box 609420
Cleveland, Ohio 44109
216-348-1825
uakron.edu./bustech/canal

The 87-mile corridor, which was designated in 1996, runs from Cleveland to Zoar, paralleling the path of a canal built to connect Lake Erie to the Ohio River. Plans call for the extension of the original canal towpath trail from the Cuyahoga Valley National Recreation Area to Cleveland's waterfront and linking of the Cuyahoga Valley Scenic Railroad Line to Cleveland's rapid transit system. Both Akron and Cleveland have water-filled canal sections.

INDEX